"The title says it all. The love that Greg and Mary Beth feel for the wild places to which they have travelled is captured in the glorious photographs and vividly descriptive text. They take us on a journey of exploration through some of the most fascinating and amazingly diverse habitats of our planet. All who go on this adventure will understand, if they did not before, why it is so desperately important that we work together to preserve the wild places for future generations. Congratulations, Greg and Mary Beth, my long-time friends."

—**Jane Goodall,** PhD, DBE
Founder, the Jane Goodall Institute
United Nations Messenger of Peace

"Leafing through the images and savoring the prose in *For the Love of Wild Places* is the next best thing to personally breathing the fragrance of a mossy woodland, catching a glimpse of a jewel-toned frog, or being surrounded by a kaleidoscope of small fishes on a tropical reef. Knowing a place leads to caring about it, and with caring there is hope that humankind will embrace wild places and the life they hold as if our lives depend on it, because they do."

—**Sylvia Earle**
American oceanographer, aquanaut, and author
Time magazine's first "Hero for the Planet"

"Greg and Mary Beth Dimijian lead readers on a thrilling journey to faraway places and others near to home using beautiful photographs and a nicely crafted narrative. There are no better guides than these two naturalists."

—**James B. Murphy,** ScD
Curator of Herpetology, Smithsonian National Zoological Park

"Greg and Mary Beth Dimijian are enormously gifted photographers and storytellers. *For the Love of Wild Places* offers readers a fascinating glimpse inside their personal four-decade journey exploring the world. Their stunning photographs and wonderful insights capture the true magic of nature and will inspire everyone to do more to protect our planet's wildlife and wild places. This is a remarkable book by a remarkable couple."

—**Michael L. Meadows**
President and CEO, Dallas Zoological Society

"In their beautifully illustrated and entertaining book, Greg and Mary Beth Dimijian take readers along on their great adventures to many of the world's most magical places. Underneath the fascinating natural history and engaging stories, there is an urgent message to all of us who imagine we will go, someday, to see these wonders and the creatures that inhabit them: go now and see them while they still remain."

—**Sean B. Carroll,** PhD
Professor of Molecular Biology and Genetics, University of Wisconsin
Author of *Remarkable Creatures: Epic Adventures in the Search for the Origins of Species*

For the LOVE of WILD PLACES

For the LOVE of WILD PLACES

Finding Adventure and Beauty in Nature

Greg Dimijian

Photographs by
Greg and Mary Beth Dimijian

For the Love of Wild Places

Brown Books Publishing Group
16250 Knoll Trail Drive, Suite 205
Dallas, Texas 75248
www.BrownBooks.com
(972) 381-0009

A New Era in Publishing™

ISBN 978-1-61254-088-7
LCCN 2013930999

Printed in the United States
10 9 8 7 6 5 4 3 2 1

For more information or to contact the author, please go to:
www.ForTheLoveOfWildPlaces.com.

This book is dedicated to my
wife, Mary Beth. Together
we have chased and caught
many rainbows.

Table of Contents

Author's Note

From the Serengeti migration in East Africa to the "Serengeti Plain" of King Penguins on South Georgia Island in the Southern Ocean, readers will journey into the intoxicating worlds of wild places. My wife, Mary Beth, and I have enjoyed countless wilderness adventures with notebook and camera in hand over the past forty years.

Each adventure story, from the tropical rain forest to coral reefs to the African savanna, is an independent narrative. A quick survey of our adventures includes the following:

- The Serengeti migration in Kenya and Tanzania, with predators and prey at close range
- The Okavango Delta of Botswana, with the animals of Africa dispersed through a "sea of grass"
- New World tropical rain forests and cloud forests, including a turtle arribada and a climb to the canopy
- Volcanoes and volcanic hot spots from the Big Island of Hawaii to Iceland
- Coral reef diving and viewing the enormous variety of life on tropical reefs
- Some of the most beautiful national and state parks of North America
- The wildlife of the Southern Ocean, from South Georgia Island to an Emperor Penguin colony on the frigid shores of Antarctica

A central tenet of the book is that the more you understand, the more you appreciate what you see.

The uncountable wildlife spectacles that Mary Beth and I have witnessed and photographed cry out for pages on which we can share them with others, before the expanding human population has eliminated the opportunity for future generations to enjoy them. We hope this narrative will be a magic carpet for all who read it.

Acknowledgments

My thanks and gratitude go to George Diggs, Henry Estess, and Bill Woodfin for their encouragement to write this book and convey to others my love of exploring and preserving natural habitats. My son, David, provided companionship and highly creative solutions for capturing photographic moments in a way that conveys the excitement of what we saw together. Bill Woodfin suggested that I include maps, even sketchy ones, to help readers visualize the places the narrative takes them. Jane Goodall has been an unceasing inspiration in the course of our long friendship; she is a world leader not only in saving our closest primate relatives but also in raising awareness of our planet's priceless natural heritage. Most importantly, I would like to thank Mary Beth for sharing the trials and rewards of these adventures, many of which were fraught with tactical challenges and real dangers. I could not have negotiated these avenues of high excitement and risk without her.

I would also like to thank the professional team at Brown Books Publishing Group. Janet Harris, my editor, enjoys skills born of twenty-five years of teaching English literature and writing at Southern Methodist University and wisely recommended that I emphasize narrative over descriptive teaching. Omar Mediano and Danny Whitworth left their indelible marks of artistry in editing the photographs and integrating them with the text. Cindy Birne reached out with great charisma and skill to those who provided deeply meaningful endorsements.

One

African Odysseys

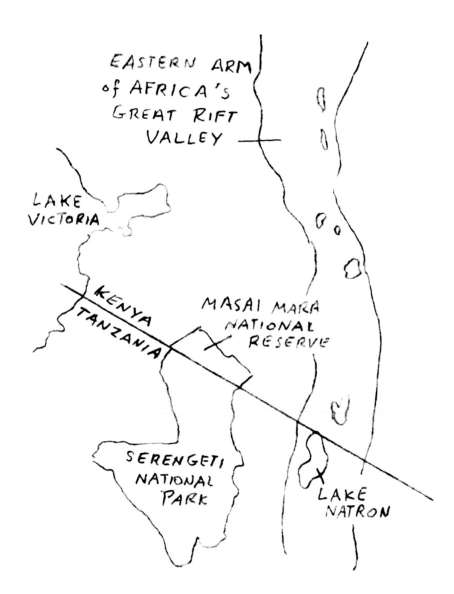

EASTERN ARM
of AFRICA'S
GREAT RIFT
VALLEY

LAKE
VICTORIA

KENYA
TANZANIA

MASAI MARA
NATIONAL
RESERVE

SERENGETI
NATIONAL
PARK

LAKE
NATRON

*The Serengeti-Mara
ecosystem is just west of the
eastern arm of Africa's Great
Rift Valley and straddles
the border between Kenya
and Tanzania.*

With a deep guttural roar, the largest lion we have ever seen rose suddenly from behind a rock only a stone's throw away. Until that moment, it had been a quiet, peaceful morning in the Serengeti woodlands of Tanzania, and we had decided to take a short stroll outside of our vehicle. I was flat on my back photographing tall grasses against the sky, and Mary Beth was identifying a bird with her binoculars. Our guide and friend Peter Davey had innocently tossed a stone at a lizard on a rock, and it had hit a lion lying on the other side.

When the lion roared, I first thought naively that it was the exhaust sound emitted by the vehicle starting. I changed my mind when I saw the huge black mane of the lion, which stood high as he cast a fiery glance at the intruders who had disturbed him. We were frozen helplessly within a few seconds' distance of a charge. As we held our breath, the lion turned and ran away. I jumped to my feet and saw two ashen-faced people racing for the safety of the vehicle. I quickly followed. When he caught his breath, Peter was furious with himself. He had broken the first rule he had taught us: never wander from the vehicle in a woodland where a lion or a buffalo might be hiding.

When he finished trembling, Peter told us what to do if we are on foot and encounter a lion which *doesn't* run away. First, we should freeze. Any movement might cause the lion to approach. If we stand still, he might turn and walk away. We should not stare at him and not raise our voices. We should then back slowly away with our arms and jacket raised or move slowly toward the vehicle if it is not in the lion's path. If the lion advances, we should consider tossing something like a camera bag or backpack at him.

"Lions know; they can *feel* if you're afraid," the famous George Adamson once said. Adamson and his wife Joy raised an orphaned lioness cub and told the story in their best-selling book, *Born Free*. Delia Owens, who wrote *Cry of the Kalahari* with her husband Mark, was alone near her vehicle in southern Africa when she was threatened by several lions. As they approached, she threw her shovel at them. The lions stopped briefly to inspect it, giving her a few precious seconds to run to the safety of her vehicle.

Wild places can be dangerous, and we have had many close encounters in Africa that we are lucky to live to tell about.

Peter was an Englishman who lived with his wife and children on the outskirts of Nairobi, Kenya. He set up a private tented camp for us in the Masai Mara National Reserve of Kenya for our first and most memorable experience in East Africa in 1974. The camp, in open woodland beside the great plains of the Mara, was maintained by four African hired hands who cooked all our meals in the camp's tented kitchen. We feasted on wild African game, including the delicious meat of giant eland, some of which was delivered personally to us from the company's hunting safaris. Peter showed us the Serengeti migration with its three migrating hooved mammals: wildebeest, Burchell's zebras, and Thomson's gazelles. He followed lions and leopards and burned into our souls the sounds and smells of the East African savanna, which we will never forget. Just the recorded sound of one bird, the Emerald-Spotted Wood Dove, takes us back to this first time on the African plains and makes us feel as if they were our primeval home.

Peter had planned for us to spend all three weeks with him in our private camp, but during the last week, I talked him into taking us to the northern Serengeti in Tanzania where the largest herds of Burchell's zebras were migrating. He reluctantly told his African staff to take down camp and go home, and we drove to the Seronera Lodge in northern Tanzania, where we moved to a hotel room instead of an outdoor camp. Our new plan turned out to be worth the sacrifice because Peter found the largest zebra herd in one place that we have seen in ten trips to Africa. I captured it in a black-and-white Hasselblad image that has sold over and over again in a Dallas gallery. In order to include the whole herd in one image, I rotated the camera forty-five degrees and took an image with the horizon extending from corner to corner of the square format. I cropped off the excess sky and grass in my darkroom when I printed it. Those shots were taken before the days of digital photography, of course, and I would have been stunned to know that someday I could just take a series of images and digitally stitch them together to create a panorama.

We learned that it was safe for us to approach almost any animal as long as we stayed in the vehicle. The quieter we were and the more slowly we approached, the closer we could get. An exception was the hippo, possibly the most dangerous animal in East Africa aside from the mosquito. We learned that if we positioned ourselves between a male hippo and his stream or pond, we risked being charged and attacked. Hippos can bite a person in two or chop off the fender of a vehicle. A male's canine teeth, used for challenging and fighting other males, are gigantic in spite of his vegetarian diet. Hippos feel safe only in the water and usually stay there in the daytime. At night, they leave their watery home to graze on the land.

Peter reminded us that we were privileged to get so close to animals in the Masai Mara and Serengeti, where they are accustomed to the vehicles of tourists and researchers. We could park close to animals, but only if we talked quietly and moved about slowly inside the open vehicle. We would not have had this privilege in many other parts of Africa, such as the Selous Game Reserve of Tanzania, where animals are unaccustomed to vehicles and flee when they see one at a distance.

There is nothing like a first trip to the East African savanna. Never have you seen such vast stretches of rolling land with uncountable animals of every kind. On any day, you are likely to see giraffes, elephants, zebras, wildebeest, gazelles of different species, hippos, warthogs, lions, and dozens of bird species, from the beautiful Lilac-Breasted Roller to the clouds of vultures that descend to fight for access to a carcass. You may see a few lions resting in a thicket of tall grass and bushes, visible only from one side of a low shrub, which is the reason you don't get out and walk across the Serengeti plains. In the early morning, at five or six a.m., you may be fortunate to watch a spotted hyena clan finishing off the carcass of the previous night's kill, with jackals darting in to steal scraps. Vultures may spot the frenzied activity from their vantage point in the sky and compete with the spotted hyenas and jackals to snatch bits of the carcass. In a nearby stream, a family group of African elephants plays in the water, drinking and spraying water over themselves; they are quick to spook and move rapidly away if you approach too closely. Masai Giraffes walk slowly across the open plain, sometimes singly and sometimes in groups of up to seven or eight; a baby is sometimes seen with them, its umbilical

Burchell's zebras from different family groups pause to drink from the Mara River in Kenya before daring to sprint across.

cord still dangling between its spindly legs. In a thicket nearby, your guide may spot a solitary leopard resting on a tree branch; it is so well camouflaged in the shadows of the tree branches that you marvel at your guide's eyesight. His eyesight may be no better than yours, but he has perfected a "search image" for animals in the landscape and learned to recognize subtle clues that an animal is there.

The Serengeti-Mara migration is the most complex land mammal migration left on the planet. In an irregular annual circle, three hooved mammals make a round-trip, following the rains and the changing grazing conditions. The zebras usually lead the way and crop the tall grass. They are not ruminants, like the other two, so they must consume large quantities of the dry, nutrient-poor tall grasses; their digestive system is said to have a high "throughput." The other two migrants, wildebeest and Thomson's gazelles ("tommies"), are ruminants like cows and sheep, and feed on the shorter and more nutritious grasses, made more accessible by the removal of the tall, stringy grasses by the zebras. It's called a *grazing succession* because the ruminants follow the zebras in succession, although this is not a hard-and-fast

As part of the great Serengeti migration, wildebeest and Burchell's Zebras rush across a shallow portion of the Mara River in Kenya.

rule. Sometimes you see all three animals together, and occasionally the ruminants go first. The animals sometimes cover the plains to the horizon, and you will be filled with a sense of awe.

There is one other large land-mammal migration on the planet, that of the caribou in the Arctic. This migration, however, involves only caribou, not three mammal species, and is thus not a grazing succession. There is another big difference between the two migrations: the African migration combines complexity and drama because of the striking diversity of mammals, birds, and reptiles, some of which are fearsome predators. The Serengeti-Mara migration should be preserved at all costs. How long will it endure the onslaught of human expansion?

This is not a trivial question. For many years, the Tanzanian government has considered building a two-lane road across the Serengeti National Park in the central corridor of the migration, in part to improve the country's access to mineral resources. This road promises to be a tragedy for the migration because it will effectively block the movement of animals across it. Wildebeest, zebras, and tommies have a strong compulsion to migrate, risking their lives crossing rivers even when they know crocodiles are waiting. They will risk their lives trying to cross the road, too. The road will eventually be fenced, gas stations and little communities will develop along it, and the migration will become history. Our friends in Africa think that little can be done to stop the government's plans. If you want to see the majesty of this unique planetary spectacle, don't wait too long.

The migration was first studied in the 1950s by a remarkable team of two people, Bernhard Grzimek, then director of the Frankfurt Zoo and professor of Veterinary Science in Germany, and his son, Michael Grzimek. They were forty-eight and twenty-three years old when they began the study. Flying a high-wing single-engine plane painted with black zebra stripes, they took aerial photos of the great herds and attempted to count the animals. In one flight, they counted 57,199 zebras on the plains. They even tried to make counts of flamingoes over Lake Natron in Tanzania's segment of the Great Rift Valley, but accurate counting was impossible because the birds would take flight at the approach of the airplane. The cinematographer Alan Root made a film of their pioneering study, but before his film was completed, a tragedy occurred: Michael, only twenty-four years old and flying alone in the zebra-striped plane, collided with a large vulture and was killed in the ensuing crash. A memorial was erected at his grave site on the rim of the Ngorongoro Crater in Tanzania, with the inscription:

MICHAEL GRZIMEK
12.4.1934 – 10.1.1959
He gave all he possessed for the wild
Animals of Africa, including his life.

The historic odyssey of Bernard and Michael can be read in their 1959 book, *Serengeti Shall Not Die*. Their black-and-white photographs archive the efforts they made and the hardships they endured. Alan Root's film of the same name appeared later and includes some of the Grzimeks' own movie sequences of the migrating herds. If a road across the Serengeti is built, *Serengeti Shall Not Die* will become a memorial to a dream lost only a half-century later, the dream of two dedicated men who believed in humanity's wisdom and conquest of greed.

I learned about wildebeest social behavior when I spent two weeks in the Serengeti and Ngorongoro Crater with Richard Estes, a behavioral biologist who has devoted decades to studying and writing about African animals. Dick described for me every nuance of their migratory and courtship behaviors. We watched wildebeest give birth in the Ngorongoro Crater and photographed newborn calves struggling to their feet. Dick considers wildebeest newborns the most precocious of hooved mammals, capable of standing and even following their mother within *minutes* of birth. A mother bonds only to her own calf, and if the calf becomes separated from her, it will not be accepted by any other female. One lost calf approached our vehicle, searching desperately for

Wildebeest fill the plains in the Masai Mara under the western escarpment of Africa's Great Rift Valley.

a surrogate mother, even if only a strange new object. All we could do was drive away and leave it to its fate. Dick told us about an orphaned wildebeest calf which was seen, for the last time, approaching a hyena.

After our first trip to the Serengeti-Mara, we resolved to return and have a vehicle all to ourselves, as reckless as that might sound. We were too excited over the idea to be appropriately worried about it. We wanted the adventure, and we had become too spoiled by Peter to consider the inexpensive option of a group safari. Peter agreed to purchase a second-hand Toyota Land Cruiser for us and lease it to his safari company during most of every year, when we would not be there.

Zero to Sixty-five in a Heartbeat

From a distance, we carefully followed the cheetah and her three nearly grown cubs for an hour. Abruptly, crouching low in the grass, she began approaching a grazing Thomson's gazelle. She began a fast run toward the tommy, which spotted her and bolted into a sprint directly away from us. What bad luck for photos. Then suddenly the tommy made a right-angle turn, and the cheetah skidded around to follow. Now was our chance! Both ran at a blazing speed across the open savanna, in perfect view of our cameras. We photographed both the cheetah and tommy in mid-air, seconds before the cheetah closed the distance and captured her prey. Her cubs ran to her side and began their feast, while their mother held the tommy's neck in a strangulation bite. The mother finally caught her breath and looked around warily for the approach of lions or other large predators.

A mother cheetah chases a Thomson's gazelle at breakneck speed on the Serengeti Plain in Tanzania.

The cheetahs had consumed their prize to the bone when vultures began dropping from the sky. A solitary lion had seen the vultures and soon arrived at the kill; the cheetahs retreated to the safety of a nearby woodland, where we watched the cubs licking blood off each other's faces. The lion picked up the tommy's carcass and carried it away.

I hoped I had gotten a perfect photo of both animals "airborne" during the chase, but the year was 1983, long before a photographer could have digital confirmation on the spot. I had to wait nearly four weeks to see the Kodachrome slide at a heart-stopping moment in front of my light table. To my relief, both animals were in focus and in the frame.

The cheetah is the fastest-running land mammal, reaching in seconds a top speed of up to sixty-five miles per hour for a short distance. It cannot sustain a long run at that breakneck speed. Only on one other occasion have we seen a full-fledged cheetah chase—in the Masai Mara in 2006. In this second instance, we were too far away to film the chase, so we just watched it through binoculars. We saw the whole event with no interruption for picture-taking and could hardly believe our eyes. The cheetah became a living streak on the open plains, moving so fast that in my fantasy I imagined it "rotating" and taking off into the air, as an airplane would rise from a runway. Instead, the chase ended in a cloud of dust, as the prey was captured.

On another occasion, we watched three cheetah cubs play in the shade of acacias north of the Masai Mara. Only one other vehicle was

Cheetah cubs play with a strange new object, a man's hat which had just blown out of an open vehicle.

there. A man's hat blew out of the open vehicle and landed close to where the cubs were playing. One cub approached stealthily, hissing, holding its ears back. The strange object was too good to pass up, but would it bite back?

The cub picked up the new, lightweight toy, and in no time, a second cub tried to pull it away. The tug-of-war was unfolding right in front of my 600-mm lens. Soon all three cubs were playing with the hat, pulling at it and tossing it around while their bored mother looked on. The game of grab, run, drop, and grab again lasted two hours. One of the tired cubs finally carried the hat some distance away and went to sleep by a log, with his paw guarding the tattered prize.

On Our Own Without a Guide

We had our own vehicle in East Africa for two memorable summers in the late 1980s. We were on our own in wild Africa and loved it, with the most extraordinary wildlife extravaganza on the planet waiting for us. It felt like being in a safe, movable cage with the largest zoo in the world all around us.

Mary Beth and I find time to relax and go over our notes in a shady grove in the Masai Mara.

Being on our own in the Masai Mara required some "basic training." Peter advised us with pointed finger that we should never drive out onto the savanna without water for us *and* for the vehicle. If our vehicle broke down, we should walk back to camp only during the day and never at night, because spotted hyenas lose all fear of humans after nightfall. We should never get out of the vehicle without a clear view of our surroundings and never walk through thick bush, even in the daytime, because of hidden lions or a solitary African buffalo. Hippos near rivers posed a serious risk. We were cautioned always to carry a compass. When off-road, we should avoid driving over acacia branches, which have long, sharp thorns that can puncture a tire, and carry a high-lift jack in case of becoming stuck in deep mud. Drivers should carry lots of spare parts, along with baling wire and duct tape, and never try to speak Swahili if stopped by the police but instead play like dumb tourists. If our vehicle was broken down and surrounded by natives, Peter advised us to "get tough" and say *no* to the inevitable demands for favors and money.

We spent each day in the field, eating our lunch in the vehicle and remaining on the ready for photo ops. We watched elephants come together from opposite directions and entwine trunks, dance around, and celebrate a family reunion. We had a photographic dream opportunity when two young male Masai giraffes performed a "necking match" display for over an hour, pressing their long necks against each other and leaning far over to one side together, like ballet dancers. We

A "necking match" between young Masai giraffe males in the Masai Mara of Kenya resembles a slow ballet dance.

knew they were practicing for mating competition with other males later in their lives. On another occasion, we watched a courting lion and lioness mate every fifteen minutes, the male grimacing and the female growling at him at the moment of sexual climax. Between matings, they rested, and if she got up and walked away, he would follow, never letting her wander more than fifteen or twenty feet away.

We stayed with this pair for only a few hours but knew that lions in East Africa typically mate repeatedly day and night for three days at a time and that a female invites many different males, not all from her

In the Masai Mara, a lion grimaces at the moment of climax.

pride, to mate with her before she "commits" her eggs to conception. She may mate hundreds of times for each of her litters. What might explain both her variety of mates and her delay in conceiving? One speculation of researchers is that she might be testing the integrity of the current male coalition in her pride, waiting to see if outside males might evict the current males. When this happens, the new males often kill young cubs, ensuring that the females will come into estrus sooner and be available to conceive the new males' own offspring—Darwinian natural selection at work. I am not suggesting that the lioness is aware of such a subtle mechanism but that genes predisposing to this behavior are more likely to make their way into future generations than genes that do not.

A mother provides additional protection to her newborn cubs by giving birth to them in a secluded place, caring for them there until they are four to six weeks old. We found a lioness in just such a secluded place nursing her two-week-old cubs and watched her from a discreet distance. We were alone with her, and she tolerated us. If we talked louder than a whisper, she would raise her ears and look at us intently. After about two hours, she walked away, at which point the cubs all took cover, an instinctive behavior which might save their lives in a land of predatory mammals, birds, and reptiles. When the cubs were older, we knew she would take them back to her pride.

Lionesses in a pride are all related to each other—not to the temporary male coalition—and tend to conceive and deliver their young at about the same time. When they bring their young cubs back to the pride after raising them for four to six weeks in isolation, the cubs may be nursed by different lactating females. A lion pride is a truly cooperative matriarchal unit. We remembered that all other wild cats are solitary; a female leopard, for example, raises her young alone, and there is no hint of social-group living in any cats other than lions, although cheetah brothers sometimes live and hunt together. All wild canines, however, are "social," living either in a pack, like wild dogs and wolves, or in a male-female partnership, like jackals. What an amazing difference between felines and canines. Do we see behavioral traces of this difference in our pet dogs and cats? You bet! Most dogs show much more emotional bonding to their owners than most cats, reflecting their evolutionary social hierarchy in the wild. Just think of the frenzied excitement your dog shows when you return from a trip.

Even though we relished being on our own with our vehicle, we missed the expert eye of an experienced guide and spent many days seeing only "ordinary" things—herds of plains animals grazing with alerted gazes, wide-open spaces with few animals in sight, and an occasional giraffe or elephant family group. We regularly spotted what we thought was a wild animal, only to discover that it was an oddly-shaped tree stump in the distance. We named one such "animal" *Stumpus girafficus*. We joked that we should write the first *Illustrated Field Guide to East African Tree Stumps*.

Driving the dusty roads of East Africa can pose a problem in a poorly sealed or open vehicle. Fine dust poured in through holes in the

The author rests his camera and 600-mm lens on a window mount of the Land Cruiser.

floor to rise and settle on us and everything in the car. We had to keep camera equipment tightly covered with plastic, and even that didn't keep the dust out. The worst times were when we had a following wind, which blew our own dust onto us.

I had installed a camera platform on the right-hand door by the driver's seat and used it regularly for supporting and stabilizing the camera, which I rested on sandbags. We rarely used a tripod in East Africa because we were constantly on the move and were usually confined to the vehicle. The window platform with a sandbag for camera support was a perfect replacement for a tripod.

Before the twenty-first century, few photographers had access to image-stabilized lenses, and film was "slow," requiring lots of light and large, fast lenses. Slide film of the late twentieth century had light-sensitivity (ISO) ratings of only 25 to 200. Photographers would have killed to have the ISO capabilities of today's digital sensors: from 25 to an unimaginable 200,000, and even higher. Image quality is compromised as the ISO moves into the thousands, but photographers can get pictures in dim light that they couldn't possibly have gotten before. Even more amazing, they can now change the ISO for each picture taken, without having to replace film.

We watched many river crossings by wildebeest and Burchell's zebras. When these animals reach a river in their migration route, they seem compelled to cross it in spite of the dangers, including deep, rushing water, crocodiles, and steep embankments on the opposite side. On a previous trip, our guide had seen a zebra disemboweled by a croc during a crossing; the unfortunate animal had managed to climb up on the far bank but then fell to the ground with its open wounds. In only a few minutes, vultures of three species were tearing at the body of the dying animal.

On one occasion, we parked by a steep bank, watching the animals cross. One wildebeest tried repeatedly to climb up a steep, muddy bank. It became fatigued as it tried and tried again, never considering another place to climb out, even though there was a gentle slope a short distance downstream. It finally grew exhausted and gave up. We assumed that it drowned as it washed downstream with the current.

Once in heavy rain, our vehicle became mired in mud, and only my limited training in four-wheel drive techniques let us resume our journey. A slow back-and-forth motion of the vehicle, with front wheels turned first to the right and then to the left, helped us emerge from a watery limbo. We were naïve amateurs in our risky quest to explore the African savanna by ourselves.

We met Jonathan Scott, now a BBC photographer, during the summer on our own in the Masai Mara. Jonathan turned out to be a wonderful friend. He showed us his special haunts and overlooks along the Mara River, where he had photographed wildebeest crossings. Willing to bend his safety rules a little, he once escorted me on foot down along the river's edge. We both knew that lions hid in bushes next to the river and that a hippo could explode out of the water and charge faster than a person can run. Mary Beth knew this, too, and sensibly remained in the vehicle. I had mixed feelings as we rounded bends in the river down by the water's edge, with cameras in hand. Without a camera, of course, there would be no way either of us would have taken those risks. As it turned out, we encountered no lions, no hippos, and no photo ops.

On another occasion, Mary Beth and I were parked in the shade of a large acacia tree by the river, enjoying sandwiches for lunch. We were all alone, or so we thought. A vehicle pulled up and stopped behind us; it was Jonathan. "Just when you thought you were alone in paradise," he said.

We shared our discouragement over finding relatively little to photograph on our own, and Jonathan reassured us that months had gone by when he had seen nothing unusual to photograph. He was sure that our animal-spotting skills would improve over time.

In the meantime, we begrudgingly decided to do as most guides do—follow other tourist vehicles, especially when several have stopped to look at something. This strategy worked well but left us feeling like part of the crowd. We struck a middle ground between going off on our own and following others.

Mary Beth's sister, Cecilia Riley, joined us for the second summer we spent by ourselves, driving our own vehicle. Cecilia is an ornithologist who created and directs the Gulf Coast Bird Observatory on the Texas coast. When she joined us, no good field guides existed for the birds of East Africa. She struggled daily with the inadequate bird plates yet managed to identify birds we had never known before. Cecilia even saved our plastic bag of exposed film from the grasp of an aggressive baboon, which had run onto the porch of our little cabin. I could vividly imagine the baboon climbing a tree with the bag of film and settling on a high branch, munching on each roll.

A Lake from Another Planet

Our light plane descended over the shallow, scorching-hot waters of Lake Natron in Tanzania, the most alkaline and caustic lake in East Africa. We had found what I was looking for: rarely seen colonies of Lesser Flamingoes, breeding miles out into the lake on soda-mud flats so hot that their mud nests were built up a foot or more above the surface, some with eggs in a depression at the top. No one knew of these colonies until the mid-1950s, when the late ornithologist Leslie Brown flew a plane over the lake and found them. Until his discovery, a local saying had been, "Lesser Flamingoes emerge fully formed from the waters of the lake." Peter Davey had given me a copy of Brown's little book, *The Mystery of the Flamingos*, which described this momentous discovery.

I had hired Angus Simpson, an expert pilot who had flown professional photographers over East Africa, to take me on a four-hour flight in his Cessna 182 with the right door off, south over Tanzania, over Lake Natron and Ol Doinyo Lengai volcano, then over Ngorongoro Crater, and finally back home over the Masai Mara.

Angus and I reached the lake after flying over the African Great Rift Valley, a zone of separation of the African continental plate and the subplate to the east. As we descended to obtain a better view of the lake, we found, to our excitement and delight, extensive colonies of flamingoes breeding on the soda-mud flats in the middle of the lake. Heat from the lake blasted us in the little plane's cabin. We descended

to 200 feet with caution, knowing that the hot air would make stalling more likely. We circled the colonies again and again, sweating in the heat and taking photos. We knew that if we stalled and crashed, we would become part of the lake's nutrient cycle. Even if we should survive a crash, there would be little chance that we could walk or swim several miles to shore across the hot, hypersaline lake. Leslie Brown had found the water temperature of the lake to be as high as 140 degrees Fahrenheit. He had recklessly attempted to walk through the shallows to find the colonies and had given up when he realized his legs were being badly burned. He needed skin grafts to recover.

I finally signaled for Angus to climb. He was exuberant and flew the plane gratefully up to 10,000 feet into cooler air and right over the top of the active volcano, Ol Doinyo Lengai. He banked sharply to the right over the crater, and I held on tight, almost dropping my camera. Spilling over the rim of the volcanic caldera was a light-gray crust, which I knew was carbonatite lava, not snow. Ol Doinyo Lengai is the only active carbonatite lava volcano on earth; this lava is composed of sodium carbonate and other sodium salts and is cooler than other

Colonies of breeding Lesser Flamingoes are scattered across the soda-mud crust of Lake Natron in Tanzania.

lavas around the world. If you are strong and daring enough, you can climb the mountain from its base and descend into its small caldera when it is not erupting. You can insert a metal ladle into the liquid lava in the crater, and it will not melt. One of our guides has led climbing safaris up the slopes of the volcano for the young and adventurous. The ash on the mountain is so thick that climbers slide back three steps for every four that they climb. The ascent is made at night, we were told, so that participants won't realize how slow their progress is and get discouraged.

Our trusty single-engine plane took us back over the northern Serengeti in Tanzania, where Angus let me take the controls, then back over Kenya, where we buzzed a lone rhino with a swooping dive and returned to Angus's tiny home airstrip.

I wondered why Lesser Flamingoes would choose such a nasty, hot place to breed. The only answer, it seemed, was that such an extreme environment provides dividends in the form of relative freedom from predators. No mammals can make it out to the nests, and probably few avian raptors ever do.

The African Night

"The African night swallows you up, and you can become hopelessly lost," Peter had warned us. We followed his advice and always had a guide with us at night. We learned that even an experienced guide can get lost, especially on a moonless night; our guide often asked a native of the region to come along.

Like a night dive on a coral reef, a night drive in wild Africa is an unforgettable experience. Animals are out that we would not see in the daytime, along with some that are active at any hour. Hippos are out of the water, foraging in the grass and among the short acacias. African wildcats, which look almost exactly like gray domestic cats, are all about, hunting in the grass. Beautiful small mammals called genets are about, often on low branches. Owls and nightjars are waking up. Herds of wildebeest may be grazing, just as they do in the daytime, but they may become confused and agitated in the glare of car lights.

We approached an enormous herd of wildebeest on one night drive, their eye reflections looking like a city of lights. Unwisely, we drove a little too close. The herd became frenzied and began to stampede in all directions as we approached, running at top speed; the sound of hundreds of hooves all around was frightening and sounded like a jet taking off. Suddenly I spotted one wildebeest running straight toward my side of the open vehicle at full speed, and I held on as it crashed straight into my door, at perhaps twenty miles an hour. It felt as if we had just collided with another vehicle. The poor beast was knocked to the ground but righted itself and ran into the door a second time. It staggered away and disappeared into the frantic herd. The door of the vehicle was dented and the handle knocked off. The Masai spotter had been shining his light in the direction from which the animal came, so it was an unfortunate example of an animal being blinded and confused by a light. A wildebeest herd would not allow such a close approach in the daytime.

Patrolling lions and hunting hyenas make the night a dangerous time for a person to be on foot. I was apprehensive when I made several "star-trail" photos, time exposures of the starry sky at night, often walking several hundred feet away from our tented camp in order to immerse the camera in darkness. When I carried the camera and tripod to the site, I could shine a flashlight in the direction I was going, looking carefully for the eyeshine of lions. But when I went back at two or three in the morning to close the shutter and retrieve the

Colorful star trails are captured from the open Serengeti Plains. Broken star trails point to a moment when the tripod was probably bumped by patrolling male lions. Acacia trees are silhouetted against a sky colored red by high dust blown from across the Indian Ocean, visible to Velvia film but not to the naked eye.

camera, I couldn't shine the flashlight ahead of me, or it would have illuminated the ground and trees captured by the wide-angle "fisheye" lens on the camera. This return trip made the hair on the back of my neck stand straight up.

I took one such photo in the remote Serengeti of northern Tanzania, and when I saw the slide after we returned home, I noticed a zigzagging of the star trails half way through the exposure. What in the world could have caused that, we wondered. Then it occurred to us: we had heard lions patrolling our campsite during the night, while the exposure was being taken. If they had wandered in the direction of the camera and bumped the tripod, it would have created the zigzag in the star trails. The photo must be the world's first "lion-modified" star-trails image.

The Okavango Delta

The Okavango Delta of Botswana is the floodplain of the Okavango River from Angola, which never reaches the sea.

Without warning, the elephant matriarch began running toward us, followed by her entire family group. Her ears were outstretched in a threat posture, and she was bellowing. "Uh, oh," our guide muttered and quickly started the vehicle. We drove away as fast as we could, with the charging elephants close behind. My son, David, barely had time to grab a camera and take a shaky video. After a minute, the elephants abandoned the chase, and we caught our breath. If our engine had not started, we would have been an easy target for elephant revenge and lucky to have survived. After it was over, we heard distant laughter across the river, where a group of tourists had enjoyed the entertainment.

Two days before the chase, we had parked our open vehicle in woodland bordering the Khwai River in the Okavango Delta of Botswana, just ahead of an elephant family group moving slowly up the stream in our direction. They were frolicking in the stream and spraying each other with fountains of water. When they were very close to us, they suddenly heard us talking, when we should have been whispering. They froze, trunks poised above, and turned slowly around. They moved rapidly away in the opposite direction. They must have remembered who had recently frightened them.

In a video frame captured by David Dimijian, a matriarch and her family group chased us along the Khwai River in Botswana. (Photo courtesy of David G. Dimijian)

Our Land Cruiser crosses a channel in the Okavango Delta. A fish-eye lens curves the horizon.

The Okavango Delta of northern Botswana is a Garden of Eden in the sands of the Kalahari Desert. Fresh water from the Angola highlands flows down the Okavango River and is trapped there, unable to reach the sea, and forms an inland delta with lush marshes, floodplains, lagoons, and islands. It is filled with the wild animals of southern Africa.

Most waterways are shallow enough for large mammals to wade across or graze in. Hippos form channels in the aquatic grass beds, and lions splash through the shallows in pursuit of prey. Elephants bathe in the waterways and wallow in the mud. African crocodiles lurk everywhere—it is not a swimmer's paradise.

In places, a dark-green sea of tall papyrus reeds blankets the delta, crisscrossed by channels that are always changing. It is easy to get lost as you thread the channels in a small boat, with the reeds towering above; only an experienced person can safely navigate the waters. We could get around most of the Okavango Delta by four-wheel drive vehicle equipped with an air intake, allowing partial immersion. We were repeatedly amazed as our guide drove right across a channel, with water coming up over the hood.

In February and March, the Okavango River reaches peak flood levels, sending a front of life-giving water down into the delta. Slowly advancing along the dry river valleys, the front moves at a snail's pace of only one mile or less per day, taking five months to travel the length of the delta. It finally arrives in the southern floodplains in August, at the beginning of the dry season. One can stand in the dry riverbeds and watch the welcome water creep slowly forward; by the next day, a dry gully has become a clear, flowing stream.

In some years, little rain falls, and the ensuing drought is devastating to wildlife. Thirsty animals congregate in huge numbers at the few water holes and mudholes. The scene is a reminder of how dependent this small ecosystem is on careful monitoring and management. Botswana faces the serious challenge of preventing excessive diversion of its precious water.

Three trips to the Okavango, each a month long, provided me with an intimate exposure to this remarkable wilderness in southern Africa. The only wildlife spectacle that I found missing was the annual migration of wildebeest, zebras, and Thomson's gazelles in East Africa.

Just the essentials—ears, eyes, and nostrils—appear above water as a male hippo guards his territory in a stream in the Okavango Delta of Botswana.

This migration is unique on the planet, and for those who have never been to Africa, I recommend that they go to the Serengeti-Mara first. If there is the option of a second trip, seriously consider the Okavango.

David accompanied me on one of the three trips to Okavango. He had designed and constructed a collapsible camera cradle for my three camera bodies and two long lenses. The cradle, strapped to the back seat, was an elegant design, enabling me to access the equipment instantly. It had a lightweight cover of sail sheeting, which kept out the fine African dust.

In stark contrast to our near miss with death during a chase by an African elephant, David and I have endearing memories of African elephants. The memories come from an elephant safari camp that allowed us to ride on the backs of tame African elephants for hours. At a lunch spot, we interacted intimately with the giants, watching them play in water with their young and letting them wrap their versatile trunks around our arms. I was especially impressed with their trunks, which are such unique tools for all kinds of activities—social interactions, pulling off leaves and branches, moving food to their mouths, smelling the air above their heads, and sucking up water or dust. The red dust is blown over an elephant's body, and the water is sprayed over the body or into the mouth. Trunks are like octopus arms, with no joints or vertebrae to divide their fine movements. It is hard to imagine having such an organ, especially as an extension of the nose. It reminded me of snakes, which can move their bodies smoothly like an elephant's trunk. But there is a difference, of course: snake bodies, unlike elephant trunks, move by means of many separate vertebrae.

A "golden shower" of baboon urine nearly landed squarely in our open vehicle when David and I were leaving camp early one morning. The baboons, high in the trees above us, were protesting our presence below their night perches. A brief whiff of the acrid-smelling liquid told us how lucky we were. Had it hit its mark, we would have been forced to make a hasty retreat back to the showers in camp.

I flew with a "bush pilot" at low altitude over the Okavango, passing over herds of elephants, pods of hippos with males fighting in a stream, mopane woodlands, running ostriches, and one hundred vultures at an elephant carcass. The little airplane, with missing rivets in the metal skin and an outdated inspection sticker, was as tattered as our vehicle in the Mara. The pilot juggled a dozen parameters at once—speed, flaps, angle of descent, bank angle, crab angle, slipping, and wind gusts. I am grateful that I am here to write about the flight.

Late one morning, David and I found nine lions sleeping in the deep shade of an acacia. We stopped at a respectable distance and waited, hoping that they would wake up and do something. We waited from 11:30 a.m. to 4:15 p.m., and they were still sleeping. We learned the hard way that lions will be lions.

In the mopane woodlands, Mary Beth and I had several close encounters with leopards, which seemed completely comfortable with our presence. One young female suddenly spotted a squirrel going up a tree and bolted up after it. In one frame from my camera and in Mary Beth's video, we caught the squirrel in mid-air above the leopard's head, leaping to another branch. The leopard lunged after it, only to miss it by inches as the squirrel dropped off the branch to the ground and to freedom. We marveled at the tree-climbing agility of the leopard, so superior to that of other large cats. Leopards often carry their prey up onto a branch, out of reach of other predators and usually unseen by

A leopard chases a squirrel in a mopane woodland of the Okavango Delta.

vultures, and enjoy consuming it in peace over several days. Leopard cubs can climb with equal agility and enjoy their mother's kill on a low branch.

The Okavango is a delicate garden in the midst of the dry savanna of southern Africa, and is utterly dependent upon the life-giving water from the Okavango River. It should be seen by anyone in love with African wildlife.

A Helping Hand for a Lost Cheetah Cub

We had never before seen a cheetah mother with six cubs. We named this beautiful animal Lucky. She moved across the Masai Mara for miles every day, her little cubs scampering along behind. The cubs were four to six weeks old and capable of keeping up, if she strolled at a casual pace. It was a challenge for us to find her each day, but our guide, Dave Simpson, had a sixth sense of where to look.

One day we heard on Dave's car radio that a lion had disturbed Lucky's family and one cub had become separated from the family. The cub was rescued by rangers who were keeping it in their custody. They wanted to return it to the family but couldn't find Lucky and her other cubs.

Dave had a hunch where to look. We drove along a ridge toward a remote valley, looking for a light-tan animal with little cubs in the vast panorama of a multicolored landscape. Abruptly Dave's keen eyes

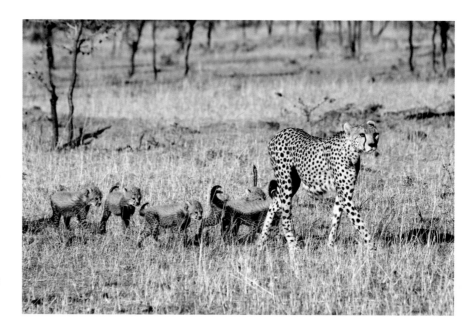

Lucky leads five of her six cubs warily through the low grasses of the Masai Mara. The four- to six-week-old cubs sport a light-colored saddle of fur that may be an antipredator adaptation mimicking the coat pattern of a small and fierce African predator, the ratel or honey badger.

Time for a playful hug for ever-watchful Mom.

spotted the family on a hidden, rolling slope several miles off-road. No one else had found them. We watched them from a distance, and they all seemed well, feeding on a gazelle the mother had killed. Dave telephoned the rangers and told them the location, and in a short time, they had joined us, bringing the lost cub wrapped in a blanket. We asked them to release the cub on our side of their vehicle to allow us to photograph the reunion. They complied and lowered the little cub in a sling over the side. To our dismay, the cub promptly ran in a direction away from the family, and Lucky had apparently not seen it. The rangers drove slowly toward the frightened cub and tried to corral it back toward the family without running over it in the tall grass, a hair-raising gamble. Again and again, the cub ran in the wrong direction. Finally, at the crest of a hill, it must have heard its mother chirping, as by now the mother had seen it and was calling for it. The cub turned toward its family and ran down the slope to join them. The family was all together again, and they sauntered away to a distant grassy slope. It was a wonderful moment we will never forget and a touching example of a helping hand offered to animals in our remaining wild places.

Spotted hyenas, unlike cheetahs, are unpopular with tourists, but their complex social behavior has made them a favorite subject for researchers. Dave introduced us to a hyena researcher in the Mara who answered many of our questions about hyena behavior. Female hyenas are larger than males and sport a large clitoris called a pseudopenis, which exactly resembles the male penis to all but other hyenas and researchers. One female becomes the dominant member of a hyena clan, and she and her cubs get the best place at the dinner table when the clan makes a kill, often in the early hours of the morning. Other high-ranking females and their cubs get second choice at a kill. Hyena fetuses are exposed to high androgen levels in the womb, and this is believed to contribute to the development of the female pseudopenis. Research is ongoing and the jury is still out, but we know that this is a very unusual mammal with a reversal of the usual male- and female-dominance hierarchy and body size. The female has a common outlet for the vagina and the bladder passing through the clitoris, as in no other known mammal. Labor and delivery are often prolonged and difficult, as seen in captive animals.

Hyena sexual anatomy has prompted some amusing and outrageous speculations in the past. In her famous book, *Out of Africa*, written in 1937, Karen Blixen, whose pen name was Isak Dinesen, quoted an "authority":

> All hyenas, you will know, are hermaphrodites, and . . . on a full-moon night they will meet and join in a ring of copulation wherein each takes the double part of male & female. . . . Do you consider . . . that it should be, on account of this fact, harder to a Hyena than to other animals to be shut up by itself in a cage? Would he feel a double want, or is he, because he unites in himself the complementary qualities of creation, satisfied in himself, and in harmony?

Like cheetahs, ostriches are among everyone's favorite animals in Africa. Ostriches are so large that they can easily be seen in the distance, even in tall grass. To our surprise, on one morning in the Mara, we spotted only the head and neck of an ostrich protruding above the grass of a broad savanna. We drove cautiously toward it and found a male ostrich sitting on a nest, consisting of only open ground in a small clearing, with an unknown number of eggs under the parent and another dozen or so eggs scattered around the periphery. It was an extraordinary sight. We quickly photographed it and left, in order to minimize our disturbance. We returned to the vicinity two days later and could see from a distance that the ostrich was still there. On the fifth day, we saw nothing through binoculars and drove slowly over to the site. What we found was disheartening: empty ground with scattered egg fragments and nothing more. Dave was angry. It was clearly the work of human poachers, he said. Nothing else would have destroyed all the eggs. A lion might take one or two, but there had been at least two dozen, and all were gone or broken. Ostrich egg shells are sold for twenty US dollars or more on the market. We photographed the sad results of human greed and left. It was the only ostrich nest we had seen in ten trips to Africa.

The animals of the Serengeti-Mara and Okavango Delta are still there in their stunning diversity, and the migration is still healthy. You must see the migration before it is disrupted by a road built across the most vulnerable part. Plan a visit to the Masai Mara between July and September to see the great herds there, with the large predators enjoying a feast after months of famine, and go to the southern Serengeti in Tanzania, such as the Ndutu area, in February or March to see the synchronized calving of half a million wildebeest. There are no spectacles in nature more awe-inspiring than these.

Under a Serengeti sky, an umbrella acacia spreads its thin canopy atop picturesque branches.

Two

Rain Forest World

On the trail, we could hear the heavy downpour coming as a roar in the forest, and we hastened to cover up. No one needed to remind us that we were in a tropical rain forest. Our arrival at La Selva, a remote research station of the Organization for Tropical Studies in Costa Rica, coincided with unusually heavy rains that persisted essentially all day long, and became torrential for ten to fifteen minutes every hour or so. A tributary of the Río Puerto Viejo, flowing in a deep gorge by the research station, rose to a level only six feet below the record high in only three hours. It almost reached the footbridge and began flowing slowly *backward*. I realized that the swollen main river must be overflowing backward into its tributaries. Pictures taken before and during the flood showed a different river, but the trees on both sides revealed it as being the same.

The trails became flooded in low areas. Researchers came back drenched, and one said, "I just gave up." Parkas are frustrating because it's hard to do anything while you're wearing them, such as take pictures, but they are essential if you want to get only wet instead of drenched. An umbrella is worthless in such rains, except to help cover the camera. I later learned that a record 129 mm (just over five inches) of rainfall had been recorded in one 24-hour period while we were at La Selva.

The forest is beautiful when wet. The huge leaves glisten with water and dance around under the falling drops. At the understory level, the forest is dark, almost black, under layers of foliage that blot out the already dim, gray sky. The rolling thunder seems to come from far away beyond the sky-tall canopy. We watch for snakes. The soil is saturated, and we walk gently on it, with the awareness that it is thin and easily disturbed; the boardwalks take on a new meaning.

The birds, hard to see even on good days, are gone now. A persistent hummer makes his rounds in moderate rain but is gone with the downpour. Presumably out there a Common Potoo remains perched atop its snag. I wonder if army ants and leafcutter ants continue their journeys, undeterred by the battering drops; do the leaf fragments carried by the leafcutters become a greater burden, to be abandoned if they are plastered to the ground?

At night the rain forest is the blackest of blacks. Our eyes play tricks on us when we turn off our flashlights—fleeting images appear and disappear, to be replaced by blackness again. Only the barest glow of a rainy sky can be discerned through breaks in the canopy. We proceed

The transcendent beauty of a cloud forest is seen from the trail in Costa Rica's Braulio Carrillo National Park.

as if blind when our light fails; the forest is spooky enough with a good light, but really scary without one.

A night walk is like a treasure hunt and reminds us of a night dive on a coral reef. Wherever a light beam falls, there may be a nocturnal critter captured in the open: a spider on a tree trunk, an eyelash viper coiled at waist level on a large leaf by the trail, or two red reflecting points in the distant darkness betraying a mammal watching intently its surroundings. As Mary Beth and I walk on the trail of the Ecological Reserve one black night, a spider about an inch long is climbing a single silken thread right in front of us; as we walk by, a small bat flies by and gobbles it up in mid-flight. For a moment, the spider is there, and in a flash it is gone. Has our light rendered it vulnerable to predation? We have heard no echolocating signals from the bat, which has flown by only two feet above our heads. Was it using visual cues only to surprise the spider?

Even the plants startle us at night. Giant, brilliant leaves of Heliconia plants loom out and shoot skyward. All of a sudden, a root

A Scarlet Macaw waits out a tropical downpour in the lowland rain forest of the Golfo Dulce of Costa Rica.

cluster dangles at the end of a liana, or woody vine, which hangs from high above. Strange forms take shape in a light beam.

The rain comes again, first audible as a whisper in the distance, and then grows in amplitude until it becomes a roar in the surrounding vegetation. We have to cover up quickly, protect the cameras, and wait it out.

On most days at La Selva, it rained only sporadically, and long hikes were possible. Temperatures were only in the seventies, but humidity was high. After an hour of easy walking with cameras and a backpack, we were soaked with sweat. We didn't want to stop walking because we would get hotter in still air. I learned to carry a bandanna to mop my brow regularly. We soon learned to re-apply mosquito repellent, as it was washed away by rain and sweat.

My backpack was soaked at the end of every day and had to be emptied and dried. Moisture seeped into my binoculars, which I stored overnight with cameras in the drying box of the lab. Everything had to be dismantled at the end of the day and spread hither and yon—camera equipment in the drying box, backpack to the rafters where a fan was blowing, other items on the adjacent bunk bed to "dry." My little voice recorder became a godsend for recording my impressions and data about photographs because a notebook was impossible to keep dry.

The researchers at the station welcomed us warmly. They enthusiastically let us photograph their projects and the animals they brought back from the field. The frogs were spectacular; one student was photographing a red-eyed tree frog, *Agalychnis callidryas,* when the colorful subject jumped up onto her camera. I couldn't resist capturing the moment.

We made a rule to share our photographs with the researchers in return for their generosity in helping us take the photos and telling us all about their research. We thus had opportunities that we could never have gotten otherwise and had enjoyable times with many fascinating people.

I heard a tree fall in the quiet, early morning. It must have been a forest giant. At first it sounded like the crackling of thunder, but thunder was out of place—there was no rain, and the sky was a uniform bland gray. The crackling grew to a roar and was followed by a thunderous thud, and then all was quiet. "Was that a tree falling?" someone asked. We all hoped no one was under it. Everyone has a fear of falling limbs and trees; it is a constant hazard in the rain forest. Heavy clusters of epiphytes ("plants on plants") on branches, especially when wet, and the shallow root systems of tropical trees make the rain forest a dangerous place. Many students wore helmets.

Once we heard the crash of a branch near us on the trail. It began with several sharp sounds like gunshots; we knew to take cover, whatever we could find, and hoped it wouldn't hit us. Branches can be huge and fall a hundred feet; we could easily be killed by one. Fallen branches provide a bonus after they are safely down: students of canopy flora and fauna take advantage of a free ticket to the canopy.

At dusk one evening, I decided to walk a few feet off-trail while following a column of army ants. In the dim light, I saw a log in their path. With the light of my flashlight, I discovered a seething mass of ants the size of a dinner plate on the log, likely the bivouac site. Ants on the surface were in constant motion, deceptively immobilized in my photographs; ants in the lower layers seemed stationary, perhaps forming a sort of framework. The returning column of ants joined the large mass by disappearing under the log at one edge of the colony. I finally felt comfortable lying on my side only twelve inches away, in order to get close pictures. Meanwhile it had begun to rain heavily, and I had to work fast because I couldn't hold camera and umbrella at the same time. I finally got the pictures I wanted and decided to blow my breath onto the colony before leaving. When I did, the entire mass was galvanized into a frenzy. Ants began pouring down in living columns onto the forest floor, forming a boiling swarm that moved toward me. I took a parting photograph and beat a hasty retreat.

In our cabin, we slept with two windows open, one on each side of the room. It rained for most of every night in June. Big drops fell on big tropical leaves, making musical sounds of different pitches. Distant thunder rumbled all night. At 5:00 a.m., we could barely make out the first light of dawn, and the constant chatter of crickets became a backdrop to the instruments of the avian orchestra warming up. It was a wonderful place for sleeping and awakening.

One time, though, I had a rude awakening. Because of the nightly downpour, I had placed my large 300 f2.8 lens on a closet shelf to protect it from rain blowing in through the screen. I awoke to find the lens much heavier than usual; it was full of water. A leak in the closet roof had been directly above it. After my initial shock, I joked that I could see a fish swimming around behind the large front element of the lens.

Arribada! Nancite Beach, Costa Rica

Darkness had fallen. I was standing alone on Nancite Beach in northern Costa Rica looking out at the Pacific Ocean. The dark sand was soft and wet, and I sank an inch into it as I walked. Our researcher friend Steve Cornelius had told us that thousands of olive ridley turtles should be homing in on this beach during the third quarter of the moon. Steve was studying the nesting behavior of the olive ridleys, which could be out in the surf awaiting the right time to come ashore. Lightning streaked the sky. The only other light was that of a lantern high up the beach near the mangroves, which cast long shadows on the sand.

Steve was taking a calculated risk in leading us from our campsite in Santa Rosa National Park to this beach by trails that took all day to hike. The arribada might not occur as expected; each month is different. We decided to take the chance and carried our food, tents, and sleeping bags. We set up the tents at the top of the beach, knowing we would have to move if the arribada began.

We awoke early the next morning to the exciting discovery that a turtle had come up during the night and buried her eggs only twenty feet from our tents in the mangrove zone. Steve counted sixty-three nests on the beach; the turtles had laid their eggs and retreated into the sea. Fifty or more arrivals in one night, Steve said, signaled the onset of an arribada, unless a heavy rain should occur the next day, delaying the arrival of the next wave of turtles. A light rain at 6:00 a.m. caused Steve to lower his hopes. Nevertheless, we moved our tents out of harm's way up into the fringe of forest above the beach. We scanned the calm ocean surface and saw one turtle head per minute come up for air. They were indeed out there.

The rain-free weather held, and we all turned in early, as darkness fell. I awoke by plan at 11:30 p.m. A bright last-quarter moon guided my short walk to the beach. I held my breath. Seven turtles were on the sand. The closest one was digging and spraying sand with wide movements of its forefeet and seemed undisturbed as I approached. Another emerged from the water, glistening in the moonlight. The sound of swishing flippers and occasional explosive exhalations mixed with the sounds of the surf.

I awakened everyone, and we watched all night as more and more turtles came out of the dark water and the beach began to fill up with

At dawn, the last of several thousand turtles were coming ashore.

turtles. We had to watch our cameras and tripods or they would be bulldozed aside and buried. Sand was thrown all over everything by the turtles—into my camera bag, shoes, even my face.

By the first light of dawn at 4:30 a.m., we could see that more turtles than ever were coming ashore. As the sky lightened, I could see and photograph the whole spectacle. Steve estimated that 5,000 to 10,000 turtles had come up in a single night.

We crawled back into our sleeping bags at 7:00 a.m. When I arose again at 11:30 a.m., the beach was mostly empty. A few turtles continued to come up, and fragments of eggshells were scattered everywhere, having been dug up by turtles making their nest in the same place as others a few hours before. From the many heads popping to the surface in the swells offshore, we knew that a large contingent of turtles still waited for the hours of darkness.

At daybreak, an olive ridley turtle emerges from the surf at Nancite Beach, Costa Rica, to lay her eggs high above the waves.

By sunset, the invasion resumed. The beach became packed with dark, resolute bodies making their way up, digging a nest, laying eggs, burying their future generations in the damp sand, and returning to the sea, like automatons. They reminded us of robots. While digging, each turtle rested periodically; if her right leg had been the last to dig, she resumed digging with her left. The nests were so close to each other that the turtles tossed sand all over their neighbors. Copious tears from their eyes left dark tracts of wet sand down their faces. The sand-covered hulks returning to the sea looked very different from the clean, glistening bodies that just emerged.

The night was overcast and pitch dark, and a cool wind brought a light rain. I was startled by a turtle that plowed into me as she made her way up the beach. A turtle's progress is slow and quiet, and if your light is turned in another direction, you can easily miss one coming toward you, even right at your feet.

The next morning dawned with almost no trace of turtles. The high tide had washed the beach clean of most of the crisscrossing tracks and fragments of eggshells. The sand was now pregnant with a half-million eggs. By 10:00 a.m., not a turtle was to be seen on the beach, but there were still heads bobbing out in the waves. The last contingent was waiting for the night, which indeed turned out to be the last night of the arribada. Steve estimated that the event was a small one for August, involving possibly 25,000 turtles.

I wondered about the eggs that were dug up by the turtles themselves. How might a strategy evolve that would reduce the likelihood of this disaster for an individual female? If a strategy evolved that called for waiting out the others so eggs would be among the last buried, what would happen when this strategy spread and more and more turtles waited out the others? It could obviously not become an evolutionarily stable strategy. Is that why no apparent solution to the problem has evolved? Or are there some individuals who actually do wait out the others, and if so, is this an unstable strategy that appears and reappears over evolutionary time, only to become maladaptive and be selected against when it spreads?

Coatis (small mammals), Black Vultures, and colorful land crabs feasted on the eggs high on the beach. When digging deep for the eggs, a coati would temporarily disappear down into the sand except for its tail and rear end and would emerge with its muzzle dripping with egg. The vultures and crabs scavenged the egg contents left behind by the coatis. To see vultures congregating at an event that is a celebration of life seemed strange.

A Volcano's Fiery Beauty

Like the other three active volcanoes in Costa Rica, Arenal owes its existence to the Ring of Fire, the subduction of tectonic plates along the rim of the Pacific Ocean. One plate, the Cocos Plate, dives beneath the west coast of Costa Rica, melting mantle rock and causing regular volcanic eruptions all along the country's north-south mountain chain. Since 1968, Arenal Volcano has erupted several times every twenty-four hours, usually doing no harm to viewers who keep a distance of several miles.

In June 1991, Mary Beth and I drove to the Arenal Observatory Lodge, located on a mountain slope only about a mile from the volcano. The lodge consisted of small rooms built originally for geologists studying the volcano, which were then available for visitors.

Just as we arrived, the volcano erupted with an enormous explosion that shook the ground, but we couldn't see anything through the dense clouds usually cloaking the volcano. After all, this part of Costa Rica is tropical cloud forest, and clouds obscure the view most of the time.

We were awakened every few hours during the night by an earth-shattering explosion. I felt a surge of excitement due to a primitive fear that we would be blown away or buried by a rain of hot ash. I knew

Costa Rica's Arenal Volcano is a cone-shaped mountain with spectacular symmetry.

we had to get outside fast, or we'd miss the show, because the sound arrived at our location some six seconds after the actual eruption.

I realized that I had to start taking a picture before the sound reached me or I'd miss half the sight. That would mean staying up all night and keeping a constant watch, trying to stay awake.

We hiked and drove around the area during the day. Over Mary Beth's objections, I ventured a short distance on foot up the flanks, and—of course—an eruption occurred. With a deafening *wh-o-o-sh-h,* Arenal shot a spectacular column of hot ash high in the sky over my head. I scrambled down the slope and humbly accepted Mary Beth's retribution.

Our last night was cloudy all night long, and we could only hear and feel the eruptions.

We left Arenal disappointed and planned to return and try again on our next trip to Costa Rica. By good fortune, we became restless during the last week of our trip and decided go back to Arenal for one night.

After we arrived, the clouds cleared, and visibility became superb. At dusk, we sat in chairs outside with cameras ready. My Nikon F4 was on a tripod with the 35-70 f2.8 lens wide open and I focused manually at night as well as I could by using a star. I had a new roll of Kodachrome 200 film in the camera, and my hand stayed on the cable release, ready to begin a time exposure at the first sight of a fireball.

Mists began to come in, and we were concerned. At 11:10 p.m. as we were almost nodding off, a small orange fireball appeared and produced a small, disappointing display. At 11:22 p.m., there was another eruption, again with poor pyrotechnics but beautiful radiating flows of incandescent rock. It came so soon after the previous one that it was another bummer.

Nothing happened for an hour and a half. We decided the next one would be a biggie. The dark hulk of the symmetrical cone was completely silent save for occasional trickles of lightly glowing rock.

Then at 1:00 a.m., a point of brilliant orange light suddenly appeared at the crater's rim and grew quickly and silently into a spectacular fireball that rose higher and higher. We both triggered our cameras on time. Streamers of rock rose hundreds of feet into the sky and arched slowly over. As the first fiery rocks started their descent, the biggest blast I have ever heard reached us. I thought my camera would be shaken by the earth-shattering explosion and would record wiggled lines starting about six seconds into the exposure, but there are no such wiggles in the image. A fire fountain filled the sky above us, and rocks rained like fireflies onto the slopes, forming rivers of incandescent rocks radiating down the mountain right in front of us. We could not believe what we had been so privileged to see so close and to photograph.

At 1:00 a.m., we photographed this eruption visible from our safe vantage point about a mile away.

I am often asked how many pictures I got of that eruption. One, I answer. I usually add that I had the entire Kodachrome roll processed without cutting, as automatic cutters often cut at the edge of the detail in a photo with a black surround.

There was another eruption at about 1:30 a.m. after we went to bed and three big ones only ten or fifteen minutes apart between 2:30 and 3:00 a.m. The middle of the three was a gigantic explosion that scared me. I imagined the manager running around telling everyone to get out of there as fast as we could. We were relieved to leave Arenal later that morning. I definitely have a residue of fear of the awesome power of that volcano.

We learned that Arenal's current sequence of eruptions had begun on July 28, 1968, with three days of catastrophic explosions that had devastated several square miles of surrounding land and killed eighty people. Since then, the eruptions have been less intense. Studies of ash deposits have revealed nine prehistoric eruptive sequences.

Earthquakes were another reminder that we were in a subduction zone of the Earth's crust where the ocean floor sinks in fits and starts beneath the continent. We have felt many small quakes since we first visited Costa Rica. When we drove along the east coast, a large suspension bridge south of Limón had collapsed and fallen into the river, and in order to cross the river, we had to drive down the sloping remains of the bridge and up a dirt road out of the riverbed.

An earthquake occurred while two of our friends were hiking on a trail, and when they returned to the field station, everyone asked them if they had felt the quake. No, they said. Then they remembered, with some embarrassment, that they had both stumbled and fallen at the same time and had just written it off to irregular terrain. The earthquake had knocked them off their feet.

Trail Adventures in the Rain Forest

A tropical rain forest trail is rapidly overgrown if trail maintenance is neglected. The trails and boardwalks in La Selva are meticulously maintained for researchers and guests. But frequently in a rain forest one encounters trails which "peter out" or divide ambiguously. For some reason—it never fails—the return path is not easy to follow, and suddenly you are lost.

This happened to me in the mountains of Costa Rica when I participated in a research project with the Organization for Tropical Studies. A slender tract of land joined La Selva to the high wilderness of Braulio Carrillo National Park, and an exploratory expedition was organized to document the flora and fauna of that tract. I was hired as the expedition photographer and physician. This experience turned out to be a daunting challenge for me and most other participants because of the steep ascents on newly cut trails.

On one excursion from camp, I became lost. My first mistake was to start out alone in unknown territory. My second mistake was to pick a narrow trail in the late afternoon. Darkness was coming soon. I continued on the trail to a river crossing and rested. After drinking a quart of water from the river, I continued on the trail on the other side, thinking I was still on the main trail. Slowly the brush began closing in on both sides. The narrowing trail frequently divided into two, and I would choose what seemed like the larger of the two forks. Suddenly there was no trail at all, and I quickly decided to turn back. Now the alternatives weren't clear. I would try one path, then turn back and try another. Finally I realized that I had lost the trail altogether. Tangled vegetation closed in on all sides, and I was bushwhacking my way through jungle, using my tripod as a very poor substitute for a machete. I had a compass and knew the direction to follow but didn't know whether to proceed toward one ridge or valley or the other. Progress in tangled growth like that is impossibly slow, and I was constantly getting caught in vines with backward-facing thorns or stumbling over logs and into unexpected holes.

Being lost like that is terrifying, especially at dusk. I was totally alone and couldn't call for help; there was a real chance that I would become more lost wherever I proceeded. I thought of going toward the river and walking in one or the other direction along it, but the brush was so thick that I could hardly make way.

Then I spotted a tree in the distance that I had photographed an hour before. I bushwhacked through the brush until the tree was the same size in my viewfinder at 90-mm focal length as before. Keeping the tree at the same distance, I moved in a circle around it; suddenly, with little light to show me the way, I emerged onto the narrow trail. I started back toward the camp, and the trail became slowly wider. Without this stroke of luck, and the photo I had taken, I would have had to make a bivouac site, stay the night, and make new guesses the following day.

I succeeded in getting lost in La Selva, too. All I did was wander off a bend in the trail, going away from the convex side of the bend. I tried to remember that if I wandered off-trail, choosing the concave side of the bend would be safer.

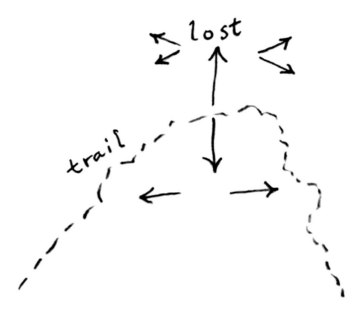

Should hikers worry even if they carry a GPS (global positioning system) receiver? Yes. GPS signals may become blocked because of obstructions, bad weather, or even bad space weather. In addition, a GPS receiver can pinpoint a hiker's location but measures travel direction only when in motion, which may not be easily achieved in an overgrown forest. A compass is therefore an important safety item, but hikers should remember that a compass points to *magnetic* north, not true north. Depending on location on the planet, hikers need to add or subtract a certain number of degrees to know the direction of true north. One website that will calculate magnetic "declination" is that of the National Geophysical Data Center of NOAA (National Oceanic and Atmospheric Administration).

The longest and most challenging trail I have taken in a rain forest was from Monteverde, Costa Rica, down the Caribbean slope of the mountains to the Refugio Eladio (Eladio's Refuge), a remote site accessible only by difficult trails. In 1996, my son, David, and I made the hike down in one day, with the guidance of our friend from Monteverde, Mark Wainwright. David carried most of my gear in a heavy backpack while I carried little, and we also used a pack mule. We descended 2,500 feet over ten miles in wet and slippery conditions.

David and I soon discovered, to our chagrin, that for every hundred feet we descended, we had to climb back up twenty-five or fifty feet because the terrain was so highly dissected by stream valleys. We would hike down a steep trail, cross a stream, and climb back up again before continuing our descent. The same was true in reverse for the return trip.

The trail took us through beautiful cloud forest and open meadows, but when we worked so hard at negotiating a trail, we had little patience to look carefully at the habitat or to search in the leaves and shadows for the thousands of little creatures we knew were hiding there.

On one stream crossing, we encountered a young couple hiking the trail on their own. The young man walked recklessly over a high and slippery log that crossed the stream, obviously showing off. Fortunately for all of us, he made it across. David, who had been trained in mountain climbing with the Mountaineers in Seattle, made an observation that never would have occurred to me: the young man was gambling with his own safety and the success of our trip as well. Had he fallen six feet onto rocky boulders, we would have had no choice but to help carry him back up the trail, along with all of our equipment, and it would have cost us two days of our short trip.

Our guide and friend, Mark, recalled a previous trip he had made to the Refugio Eladio. The hike had begun in good weather, but clouds soon brought torrential rains, and river crossings became a flirt with death. One hiker tried to cross a river after dark and got swept away; he somehow grabbed hold of a rock and clung to it, with the current

David and I crossed this placid creek near the end of an all-day hike down the Caribbean slope of Costa Rica. The setting was undisturbed rain forest cloaked in deep green.

smashing against him and sending torrents up both sides of his head. Mark couldn't reach him and didn't dare go in to help him. In the light of a flashlight, Mark saw him make a desperate lunge to reach the shore, and he barely made it. The others also tried to cross and found that in the light of a flashlight the rushing water was disorienting. A flashlight provides tunnel vision, and all you see is rushing water. You can't see bottom or the woods around you. Crossing a rushing stream at night is a risky gamble.

The others finally found a safer way to cross but couldn't find the trail on the other side of the river; they learned the hard way that trails often resume at a point not exactly across from where they end at a river. They had to give up reaching the refuge that night. Wet and cold, they tried to sleep by huddling together and putting a large palm frond over their heads. They reached Eladio's cabin the next morning after a close call.

Fortunately David, Mark, and I encountered no such rainstorm and reached the cabin by nightfall, ready for a week of hiking in the completely wild forest.

A red-eyed treefrog in the lowland rain forest of Barro Colorado Island, Panama, clings to a plant stem at night.

The tropical rain forest, unlike the open plains of Africa, provided wonderful opportunities for finding small, hidden animals. Colorful frogs and insects were everywhere. They were often in dark places, so strobe photography at close range was needed. I used two strobes to prevent harsh shadows on either side of the subject. David had designed and built a macro bracket that held the camera and two strobes, and it proved to be a marvel for capturing shadow-free macros of anything that moved or didn't move. I found that I could also use the macro bracket with strobes for distant objects, such as monkeys in dark forest or up against a light sky.

When looking at the stars at night, David remarked that we were even more remote from civilization than we had been in the Okavango Delta because we had hiked to the cabin on foot and had to leave the same way. We heard no sounds of civilization other than a remote jet flying far overhead.

Back from our arduous hike to Eladio's Refuge, we were treated to a private hike with Wolf Guindon on a remote Monteverde trail. Wolf, one of the Quaker founders of Monteverde, was a master of trailblazing and often spent the night in the forest while mapping out a new trail. He told us that if we tried to cross a swollen river, there may be another one, or a branch of the same one, to cross afterward. In such a case, we might become stranded between the two with the water rising.

Wolf had been the first and last person to see the golden toad, a beautiful amphibian that he had helped me photograph in 1989. That was the year that he saw the last one. No one has found them since, and we are all saddened by their almost-certain extinction. They had occupied only a small fragment of the wet montane forests above Monteverde and were vulnerable to human disturbance and climate change.

A masked treefrog in the cloud forest of Peñas Blancas, Costa Rica, seems to be strumming a stem.

These beautiful golden toads were photographed in the cloud forest of their only known home, Monteverde, Costa Rica, in 1989, the year they disappeared. The tiny population is now believed to be extinct.

Tropical Biodiversity

The tropics are home to a staggering variety of plant and animal species. Before his untimely death in a plane crash, the legendary tropical botanist Alwyn Gentry documented 300 species of woody plants in just one hectare (about two and one-half acres) of lowland rain forest in Peru. That compares to about thirty-five species of woody plants found in one hectare of the richest temperate forests in North America, such as the Smokies. The same astronomical increase in species numbers occurs in insects, amphibians, reptiles, birds, and mammals, as we go from temperate to tropical latitudes. What can explain this?

One guess, the "species-energy hypothesis," proposes that the tropics provide more energy in the form of more sunlight and food availability throughout the year than temperate forests. How this might contribute to *growth* is easier to understand than how it can explain *diversity*.

Another hypothesis states that greater structural complexity of plant roots, trunks, and branches in the tropics creates more diverse small habitats for more insect species to specialize in. This is technically called "fine niche partitioning." If there are more insect species, maybe vertebrates that feed on insects can specialize, too, resulting in more species of amphibians, reptiles, birds, and mammals. In other words, diversity begets diversity. But what explains greater *plant* diversity?

We found that in tropical rain forests we often had to walk a hundred feet or more along a trail to find a second tree of the same species. This surprised us because in North American forests we had often found a stand of trees, all of the same species, growing together. This feature of tropical forests has generated still another hypothesis for tropical biodiversity, one that addresses plants. Why would a plant "want" to grow at a distance from others of its own species? Research has shown that in both tropical and temperate forests, but especially in tropical forests, plants often survive and grow better if not clustered together, because of pathogens, parasites, and seed predators unique to that species. By growing farther apart, two plants of the same species can avoid *sharing their enemies* as intimately. We decided that these plants are just like us. We keep our distance from someone who has a cold.

One final guess about tropical biodiversity involves the virtual zoo of codependent or mutualistic relationships in the tropics, which could easily multiply the number of plant, animal, and microbial species. We

A hard-working leafcutter ant in Costa Rica cuts a segment out of a leaf, and is attended by two smaller caste members waiting to ride the leaf fragment back to the nest to protect the larger worker from tiny parasitoid flies. This image was used for a Costa Rican stamp (below).

have spent many hours watching leafcutter ants carrying leaf fragments back to their huge underground nests and often wondered what that subterranean world was like. A friend in Monteverde who owns a butterfly garden dug up a leafcutter nest and placed it in a glass chamber with entry and exit holes for the ants. We could see the ants come and go, as if the nest were still underground. Mutualistic fungi covered the soil of the nest, and we could see the ants bringing leaf fragments to the fungi for food. The fungi, in turn, produced a secretion that served as food for the ants. The two organisms, one an insect and the other a fungus, utterly depended on each other. When an ant queen leaves her home to start a new nest, she must carry with her some of the fungus, along with her eggs, or the new nest will never succeed. Genetic studies have shown that leafcutter ants and fungi have depended on each other for fifty million years. It has been an enduring partnership.

Another researcher, Cameron Currie, found a third mutualist in a leafcutter mutualism, and he became the envy of ant researchers everywhere. He was looking at some whitish discoloration on the thorax of one of his ants when he decided to try to culture it, and he

In pouring rain, a procession of leafcutter ants carries leaf fragments back to their nest, with smaller caste members riding the leaves.

found that it was a *Streptomyces* microbe of the kind that produces many of the antibiotics we use in medicine. He knew that leafcutter colonies are often attacked by a pathogenic or disease-causing fungus that kills their fungal partner, so he acted on a hunch and exposed the pathogenic fungus to the *Streptomyces*. His hunch paid off: it killed the fungus. It might, then, serve both the ants and their fungi as a third mutualist. His scientific paper, published while we were in La Selva, argued that this is actually a three-way mutualism, with three partners that have coevolved over long evolutionary periods. Since his discovery, many other three-way mutualisms have been found in plants, insects, and fungi. The closer we look, the more unexpected wonders we find in biology.

Fungi can thus be "friends" or "enemies" of leafcutter ants. Another fungus, *Cordyceps*, is a known enemy of its ant host; the ant dies from the infection, but just before it dies, it is programmed by the fungus to climb a short distance above the ground on a tree or a leaf stalk, where it anchors itself to the plant surface with its jaws. The fungus then forms a whitish stalk rising from the ant's body and broadcasts its spores to the wind.

A marine biologist friend of mine once asked me, "Greg, how many habitats are there?"

I answered warily, "Well, let's see, there's land, freshwater, saltwater . . ."

"What about a fourth?" he queried.

I was stuck. I had been taught in Ecology 101 that "habitats" are environments like forests, deserts, and oceans. "How about a host?" he asked. I finally understood that this fourth "habitat," a host body that another organism lives in or on, may be the most common habitat of all. I realized that the term "ecology" had taken on a new dimension.

The fig-wasp mutualism illustrates this "fourth habitat" and turns out to be one of the most unusual coevolutionary "handshakes" between organisms. Most tropical figs rely on a tiny wasp for pollination, and the wasp in turn relies on the fig "fruit" for its own reproduction. We knew it would be tricky to photograph. We enlisted the help of our friend Bill Haber, a biologist who lives in Monteverde. Bill took us on a hike to find a fig tree with unripe fruit. As I ducked under a low branch on a steep trail, Bill said, "Stop and look over your head." Startled, I thought a snake or something was right above me. Instead, it was a tree branch laden with unripe figs. We collected a sack full and headed back to our cabin, where we spent the rest of the day cutting the figs open with a razor blade and making macrophotos of the spectacular sight inside: dozens of tiny wasps and hundreds of tiny fig flowers. The fig

Tiny fig wasps emerge from an unripe fig just after the fig is cut open. The figs, less than an inch in diameter, were collected from a wild fig tree in Monteverde, Costa Rica.

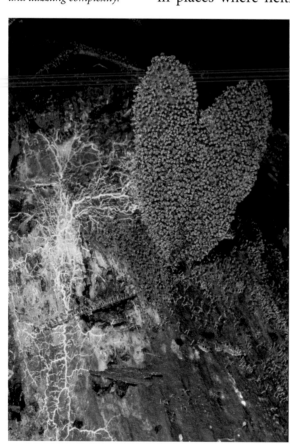

Like nothing else on earth, a plasmodial slime mold advances over a rotting log and heart-shaped leaf in the tropical rain forest of Costa Rica. The branching yellow "slime" (plasmodium) on the log climbs the leaf, drips off (image on front cover of book), and magically transforms itself into a Lilliputian forest of tiny individual fruiting bodies called sporangia. The plasmodium, a soup of nuclei that can pass through a piece of filter paper unchanged, has metamorphosed into a multitude of stalked bodies on the leaf and nearby log. A primitive organism is revealed as a thing of beauty and dazzling complexity.

itself is an unusual structure that we usually call the "fruit": instead, it is a combination of internal flowers and fruits utilized by the wasps for their own reproduction and relished as food by birds and mammals, including humans. Fortunately, the wasps have all left by the time the fig ripens.

In mutualisms such as this one, natural selection has been shown to act on each partner individually. Even though both partners mutually benefit each other, there is nevertheless an evolutionary standoff over time. If one partner takes advantage of the other or neglects to provide "services" to the other, the mutualism suffers, with the defaulting partner being rejected or replaced by another species. The relationship between any two partners is thus dynamic.

One particularly stable mutualism is that of lichens. Found the world over, they are a mutualistic symbiosis between a fungus, which provides scaffolding, and an alga or a cyanobacterial species, which lives inside the scaffolding and provides nutrients through photosynthesis. The two partners in the lichen mutualism can grow in places where neither can survive alone, and there seems to be

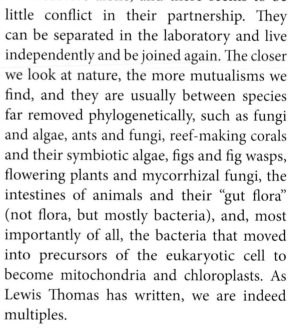

little conflict in their partnership. They can be separated in the laboratory and live independently and be joined again. The closer we look at nature, the more mutualisms we find, and they are usually between species far removed phylogenetically, such as fungi and algae, ants and fungi, reef-making corals and their symbiotic algae, figs and fig wasps, flowering plants and mycorrhizal fungi, the intestines of animals and their "gut flora" (not flora, but mostly bacteria), and, most importantly of all, the bacteria that moved into precursors of the eukaryotic cell to become mitochondria and chloroplasts. As Lewis Thomas has written, we are indeed multiples.

The neotropical avifauna is the most diverse in the world. Our friend Wolf Guindon and his wife Lucky have seen seventeen different species of hummingbirds come to their feeder in their home just outside of Monteverde. The Resplendent Quetzal, considered by some the most beautiful bird in the world, is common in Monteverde and other cloud forests of Costa Rica, and a drawing of a male embellishes the one-quetzal note of Guatemala. With Wolf's help, I managed to get close to a quetzal nest. The male flew into the nest. His tail was so long that he could take only part of it in with him; he turned around and stuck his head out, with his tail protruding out beside his head. On one attempt to photograph a quetzal high in a tree, I set up my tripod with a camera, a 600-mm lens, and three strobes on a steep slope, and lost my footing. Head over heels, I tumbled down the slope, with the camera falling over the tripod. Then I picked up everything, and tried again.

My most memorable and miserable bird-watching experience in Monteverde was of Long-tailed Manakins at a lek site. A lek site is a mating arena, in this case on a thin, low branch where two males perform a dance ritual. I knew the birds were in the forest and waited for nearly two days for them to dance. I sweltered beneath my camouflaged poncho, which I used as a blind. The two males were perched near me, singing their "to-le-do" duet, the first and last notes sung by one male, the middle one by the other.

His long tail feathers protruding above his head, a male Resplendent Quetzal perches at the opening of his nest in a dead snag (remnant of a tree trunk) in the Monteverde Cloud Forest Reserve, Costa Rica. Wolf Guindon took me to this special nest site right in the reserve.

On the second day, I was ready to give up, when suddenly the ritual dance began. It was mesmerizing. While vocalizing, the two males would stand on the branch and jump over each other in a graceful arc. I could barely make out a female watching discreetly at the edge of the stage. The lek dance terminated in the female's choosing to mate with one of the males; it was probably the dominant or "alpha" male. I learned that the "beta" male may spend up to ten years performing as a subordinate and may be rewarded by inheriting the alpha male's place if the latter dies. I was lucky to be one of the first photographers to get images of a lek dance and mating episode. A researcher had waited for a year to publish an article on Long-tailed Manakins, and when a friend of ours told *Natural History* that I had images, they called me and published the images with the researcher's article the very next month.

Considered one of the most beautiful birds in the world, the male Resplendent Quetzal rests in a tree in a forest clearing next to the Santa Elena Reserve in Costa Rica. This male has an unusual blue color in his wing and tail feathers.

My luck held out for getting photos of another rare sight right off the trail in La Selva. A researcher led David and me to a low Heliconia plant with folded, "tented" leaves, and told us there were some white "tent-making" bats hiding there. I crept over to the leaves, which were only five feet above the ground, and found the bats huddled together on the underside of the leaves, resting. They didn't move. I slowly positioned the camera with two strobes and took a picture.

Tiny white tent-making bats rest on the underside of a large Heliconia leaf, only a few feet above ground, in the lowland rain forest of the La Selva Biological Station, Costa Rica.

Unfortunately, I was at the end of a roll of film. The motor drive began automatically rewinding the film, and I could hear David softly groan. I crept slowly away, put a new film in, and tried again.

After getting the picture, I had time to think about what I had photographed. These were tiny, beautiful bats with white fur and pink faces, and they had chewed the midribs of a large Heliconia leaf to make a tent over their heads that sheltered them from tropical downpours and hid them from most predators. I later learned that one of the bats' predators, white-faced capuchin monkeys, had developed a "search image" for tented Heliconia leaves in the lowland rain forest, dropping to the ground and looking underneath the leaves for bats. They would jump up from the ground and grab them for a tasty snack.

White-faced capuchin monkeys express curiosity when looking at us from their perch above a steep, forested valley in Monteverde, Costa Rica.

Climbing to the Rain Forest Canopy

I strapped myself in the harness and snapped the jumar ascender clamps in place. My climber friend and teacher, Jim Beach, stood by, as Mary Beth looked on.

A tiny squirrel monkey leaps from a branch eighty feet above us with her juvenile clinging tightly to her back.

"Now start up," Jim said. I inched up the rope a short distance, rotating helplessly as I left the ground. "Now come back down," Jim instructed. "I'll go first, and you know how to join me up there." *Up there* was a wooden platform one hundred feet off the ground, built into the sturdy crotch of a huge rain forest tree in La Selva.

Jim made the climb in no time, and I could barely see him through the foliage as he moved off the rope onto the platform. I knew it was time for me to go up. Scared to death, I climbed slowly, trying not to look down. I waved goodbye to Mary Beth when I was high above her. It began to rain and then to pour. I must have been halfway up when I realized I could hardly see the ground. I could, however, make out the buttressed tree roots directly below me and calculated that I'd hit them at fifty miles an hour if I fell. *Why am I ending my life in this way?* I asked myself.

After what seemed an eternity, I saw Jim leaning over the platform a short distance above. Breathless, I climbed up to him and clung to the wet platform as I edged my way onto it.

When I regained my composure, I peeked over the edge. All around and below was a lush tropical forest glistening in the rain. Great canopies of palm fronds opened their graceful rosettes in the lower canopy halfway down. Moss-draped lianas, or woody vines, hung in wide arcs from tree to tree. Epiphytes dropped their long roots to the ground below.

Jim told me that the platform had been used almost daily by a researcher studying bird behavior in the canopy. He reminded me that the canopy harbors the greatest diversity of plants and animals in a tropical forest. For biologists, it is a candy store, a frontier of exploration and research.

I remembered that wherever there is a large strangler fig, it is possible to climb to the canopy without a rope by climbing up inside the root cone of the tree. I once climbed only a few feet in this manner, marveling at the spacious inner world where a host tree had once been. A strangler fig that begins its life as an epiphyte sends down a network of roots that encircle the trunk of the host tree, growing thicker after they reach the ground. The host tree is strangled and eventually dies.

The root cage of a tropical strangler fig becomes a hollow cylinder after the host tree dies and decays. Viewed from inside the base, it is now the sturdy trunk of the fig tree.

After it decays, the fig tree has a hollow trunk that extends high up in the forest.

I asked Jim if he knew Nalini Nadkarni, an intrepid biologist friend of ours who had become as nimble as a monkey, climbing trees with the jumar-ascender technique and carrying up with her a hammock, which she would hang under a strong branch high in the canopy. She would lie in the hammock all day, looking at everything that moved. She also discovered canopy roots, which earned her a spot on the cover of *Science* magazine. Canopy roots are real tree roots that grow out of the tree trunk high in the tree, tapping into the food and water in soil that accumulates in the canopy. The roots are just like the roots that extend below the ground at the base of the tree. No one had known this before, and the discovery enriched the field of ecology with knowledge about a new route of nutrient recycling in forests.

When I was hiking once with Nalini on a trail in La Selva, we came across a large fallen branch festooned with epiphytes. I asked her to show me the canopy roots. She peeled back a layer of root-matted soil on the branch and revealed thin roots emerging from the wood of the host tree.

After Jim and I had enjoyed the view, he told me to descend first. He checked my rig and said, "Go." Stepping off the platform and committing my fate to the rope was one of the scariest things I've ever done, but once I was on my way down, I lost all fear. The slow free fall was exhilarating as I glided through the palm fronds, closer and closer to the ground. When I touched down, I kissed Mother Earth.

Three

Volcanic Hot Spots

The danger of visiting volcanic areas can enhance their appeal. We were close to Arenal Volcano in Costa Rica when it erupted but just far enough away to be reasonably safe while experiencing awe. We were close to gentle volcanic eruptions on the Big Island of Hawaii, even while camping alone near a lava flow, and were just afraid "enough" for the experience to be spine-tingling and unforgettable. In Yellowstone, we hiked with others above an enormous volcanic plume in the earth but saw only the spectacular thermal features resulting from heat rising to the surface. In Iceland, we saw landscapes sculpted by violent volcanic eruptions in the recent past but were never in any apparent danger. In Africa's Great Rift Valley, we sweltered in the heat of a spreading rift in the continental crust.

The restless surface of our planet was never more palpable than in our travels in Hawaii, Yellowstone, and Iceland.

The Big Island: Living on a Volcano

Fiery fountains bubbled along the walls of Pu'u O'o crater as our helicopter approached the rim. With the right door removed, I could gaze straight down onto the grinding plates of the lava crust, searing heat radiating from the cauldron.

Lava spilled over a low point in the rim of the lava lake and formed incandescent streams moving slowly downhill toward the Pacific Ocean. The streams soon became covered with cooling crust, giving

Hovering above the lava lake of Pu'u O'o Crater, we stay just above the edge of the crater rim in case of engine failure. A fish-eye lens captures the helicopter cockpit with Mary Beth and our pilot.

birth to lava tubes. The slopes of Kilauea Volcano on the Big Island of Hawaii have been covered many times with lava flows that left lava tubes forming long tunnels beneath the ground.

The crustal plates on the surface of the lava lake reminded us of continental tectonic plates on a small scale. Some would slide alongside each other, and others would bump into one another to form a crumpled zone of lava. One plate would even "subduct" beneath another, just as much larger continental plates do. We tried to capture the unforgettable sight on Velvia film, a good way to photograph subtle colors and contrasts before digital photography made everything easier. The heat from the lake made us realize how dangerous it would be to carry out our tentative plans to hike up to the crater rim.

Dangers aside, the following week we backpacked ten miles to the crater with a tent. On the advice of rangers, we carried gas masks that would hopefully protect us if we were enveloped during the night with a cloud of toxic gases from the volcano. A friend later joked, "You couldn't even kiss each other good-bye!"

Crustal lava plates in Pu'u O'o Crater are outlined in incandescent orange, sliding past and under each other like continental plates of the Earth's crust. Erupting lava adds to the plates at one point along the walls. In the distance is the coastline of the Big Island.

Deep in a lava tube, Mary Beth lights the way under a maze of hanging roots produced by trees on the ground surface above the roof. Cave-adapted invertebrates thrive on the nutrients provided by the roots.

small for you to pass through near the end. Human bones and burial ornaments have been found in the deep recesses of some lava tubes.

There are many easy and scenic hikes over the primeval landscape of the Big Island. One not to miss descends from the rim of Kilauea Iki Crater down onto the crater floor and climbs back up again, for a total vertical distance of 400 feet, about the equivalent of a thirty-story building. That sounds like a strenuous hike, but with the excellent trail system of Hawaii Volcanoes National Park, it is easy if you take your time. We hiked in a light, misty rain, which made the undulating crater floor mysterious and beautiful. It was like walking through a fog on a frozen, chaotic sea. All eruptive activity had occurred long ago, and the lava was solid and cool. Solid, perhaps, except for the roofs of lava tubes that were usually too thick to fall through, but we walked off the trail with caution. You can usually tell when you walk over a thin roof because footsteps sound hollow. Even though the lava floor would not be hot, it might be six feet down.

The monotonous gray color of the lava floor was punctuated by the bright-red flowers of ohia lehua saplings, which eked out all the nourishment they could from the sparse soil. As we climbed out of the crater, we re-entered the forest that had grown around the crater long before it had been created.

On another crater hike, we found little strands of golden "Pele's hair" blown by the wind against the base of small plants growing on the lava surface. These tiny, beautiful filaments are golden-colored threads of lava that congeal in the air as they are ejected and are so delicate that they break if picked up. They are best left in place and photographed. A careful search found many small forms of lava rock, including some that glittered like jewelry and a featherweight piece that had solidified with a high content of gas bubbles and looked like a piece of stiff gray foam.

On yet another trail on the flanks of Kilauea Volcano, we climbed to the top of a small island of forest that had been spared burial by a lava flow which had passed by on either side. Called a kipuka, such a remnant of vegetated landscape was once part of a larger landscape now covered with lava. After this trip to Hawaii, when we had returned home to Dallas, I happened across some color slides I had taken during our helicopter ride over the same area many years before. From the air, the kipuka looked like a ship afloat in a frozen gray ocean. In some of the images,

The colorful young frond of a Sadleria *fern brightens the gray lava landscape of the slopes of Kilauea Volcano on the Big Island.*

I could see fresh lava pouring out of a "perched lava pond" located upslope only a few hundred yards from the kipuka and realized that at that time, the lava ocean must have been fairly fresh, possibly even still warm. We felt a pang of envy for residents of the Big Island who can watch their dramatic landscape evolving from one year to the next.

Some old lava flows have become overgrown with a thin crust of a gray lichen called *Stereocaulon*. It forms a miniature forest over a rough and fragmented lava field and is home to scattered ohia lehua saplings. Lichens are made up of a fungal matrix with embedded photosynthetic algae or sometimes cyanobacteria. They are a mutualistic association between two very different life forms that have coevolved because of benefits they confer on each other. The fungus provides a substrate, and the algae or cyanobacteria provide food by virtue of their photosynthetic ability. Lichens often grow on harsh substrates before any other organism can. They are classified as separate species even though they are a combination of two different organisms. A lichen can be teased apart in the laboratory and either of its component organisms

Ohia lehua trees and an understory of tree ferns grow in a rain forest on the Big Island of Hawaii.

can sometimes survive on its own. We knew that the lichen forest on the lava would eventually form a thin layer of soil in which a taller forest of flowering plants would grow.

Beaches on the Big Island are as varied as the volcanic landscape. Some are formed of quartz sand, others of deep-black basaltic sand, and still others of greenish olivine sand. Beaches alternate with steep, rocky cliffs. The Hawaiian Islands are battered by huge waves born of a 2000-mile "fetch" of open ocean, where they grow from relentless wind pressure. From rocky cliffs, we watched monster waves break on cliff faces and bounce back to sea as returning waves, colliding with incoming waves to burst into geyser-like columns of spray shooting skyward. The islands are a dream destination for surfers, who risk life and limb to ride dangerous and exhilarating waves.

Had Darwin visited the Hawaiian Islands, he would have seen a flora and fauna even more isolated than that on the Galapagos Islands, which are only 600 miles from the coast of Ecuador. Fewer species reach more isolated islands, and the few that do are random winners which have been blown there, have ridden ocean currents, or have been brought by birds. They have few competitors or predators at first, and can thrive and evolve into a radiation of new, endemic forms. Islands are "laboratories" of evolution. The Hawaiian Islands were once a living museum of unique and wonderful endemic life forms, from the mountaintops to the shores. Today this is far from what we find on the islands. Human settlers introduced a host of alien species of plants and animals, including mosquitoes. The original flora and fauna share the land with many exotic species which easily overwhelm endemic ones, especially in the lowlands. Beautiful, multicolored tree snails of the genus *Achatinella* used to cover the trees like Christmas ornaments but have been all but eliminated by a large predatory snail introduced to control another invasive snail. Birds have suffered a similar fate; the Bishop Museum in Honolulu preserves specimens of extinct honeycreepers with spectacular specialized bills that once were abundant on the islands. The many birds introduced by humans include the Japanese White-eye, Northern Mockingbird, Barn Owl, Mourning Dove, Northern Cardinal, and House Sparrow. Several human generations ago, it was easy to see native Hawaiian birds. Now you see mostly foreign birds. In our planetary conquest, we are making "McEcosystems" of most lands and habitats.

On our earlier trips to Hawaii, we were fortunate to spend time with the late Bill Mull, a research associate at the Bishop Museum who made landmark contributions to Hawaiian natural history. He had a way of explaining things that a child could easily understand. He explained island biodiversity for me, and my notes record an approximate but unforgettable quote:

> The Hawaiian Islands are Mother Nature's most dramatic declaration of independence. Big Mama looked at the world and said, "Let's try something new." But you can't try very many new things on the continents; there just isn't room for it. Most niches have been filled and it would be hard for a newcomer to make a go of it. So Big Mama chose a blank spot in the middle of the Pacific Ocean and said, "OK, here you are, here are some brand-new islands without anybody there." She let different creatures reach this safe, uncluttered place by whatever means they could. She then said to these newly arrived plants, insects, spiders, and birds, "Now let's see what you can do!" And you see around you what they all did.

Ticking Time Bomb: Yellowstone National Park

As we started out at daybreak in January, 2011, the rear-view mirror in our snowcat recorded the outside air temperature as *minus twenty-three degrees Fahrenheit*. An ice fog lay low over the snow-covered road as we drove deeper into Yellowstone National Park. Frosted bison grazed along the river, and at one point, they chose to cross the shallow Madison River. The water heated by thermal springs upstream was warmer than the air temperature above it. The rising sun lit the mists over the winding Gibbon River and created scenes of magical beauty, with snow-covered trees and a lifting fog. In the Porcelain Geyser Basin, there were dozens of fumaroles (steam vents) pumping steam and gases at high pressure into the cold air, providing a much more spectacular show of steam and mist than is seen in the warm air of summer. One large steam vent had built around itself a circular ice wall that resembled a crater, which would melt when the weather turned warmer. Small lodgepole pines enveloped in steam became "ghost trees" completely cloaked in ice, their branches bending over like the arms of a ghost.

Yellowstone, our country's first national park, rests atop the largest "hot spot" (called a *mantle plume*) of any continent, a body of partly molten rock extending many miles below ground. The mantle plume has pushed Yellowstone up more than 1,000 feet higher than it would be if it were, say, a few hundred miles farther north or south along

An icy early morning fog cloaks the slopes above a small group of bison grazing through openings they have made in the snow in Midway Geyser Basin of Yellowstone National Park. The early dawn temperature in January was minus twenty-three degrees Fahrenheit.

the Rocky Mountain range. Yellowstone is a ticking time bomb which has blown its top three times in the past two million years. The last large eruption, some 640,000 years ago, left an enormous caldera that encompasses a large fraction of the park and underlies the hottest thermal features. Its walls have been partly eroded and obscured by smaller subsequent eruptions so that it is hard to see the walls unless you fly over the region. Most people driving or hiking in the caldera never realize they are inside a living, breathing supervolcano.

The land over the hot spot is undergoing what geologists call "inflation" and "deflation" in real time, slowly expanding a few feet upward and deflating a few feet downward as the plume delivers lava and heat upward or as the ground releases water and steam from surface vents. The likelihood of another major eruption, however, is considered slim for many thousands of years; volcanoes "huff and puff" for long periods before erupting. In the meantime, we are privileged to see, close up, the most extensive geothermal activity on the planet—hundreds of slowly wandering fumaroles, geysers, and thermal springs, many of which change location from one year to the

Bison move through a plume of steam rising from a warm stream in the Lower Geyser Basin of Yellowstone.

A long-tailed weasel in winter pelage pauses for a moment as it races back and forth on the banks of the Madison River in Yellowstone. The coat color of this beautiful little mammal changes to a warm brown above and deep yellow below in the summer.

next. In the winter, with air temperatures below freezing, the thermal basins such as Norris and Porcelain Basins are places of ethereal beauty. Vents spray boiling water like fire hoses into the air. In some places, the ground is hot and dangerous to walk on. In the same way that thin lava crust in Hawaii can break under your weight, so can a thin crust of ground in Yellowstone's geyser basins give way, dropping you into a cauldron of superheated water.

Yellowstone's hot spot starts at depths as shallow as a few miles and extends several hundred miles below the surface. Geologists think it has remained stationary while the North American plate has moved west-southwest over it, an inch or two a year, forming the Snake River Plain, a lava-covered landscape extending through part of Idaho, Nevada, and Oregon. This swath of past volcanic activity is covered with layers of dark lava formed of basalt, which has obliterated the earlier calderas formed when the hot spot was beneath the plains. Just as the Big Island of Hawaii and the baby underwater volcano Loihi are at the leading edge of the Hawaiian Island chain, so is Yellowstone at the leading edge of the Yellowstone hot-spot trail.

We came upon isolated stands of dead lodgepole pines in the thermal basins, where volcanic heat is close to the surface. The trunks of the pines were silhouetted against a "whiteout" of steam clouds beyond, creating a monochrome canvas of geometric art. The pines had been killed by migrating regions of heated water in the soil of the geyser basin they once thrived in. Some trunks are called "bobby-sox trees" because of a skirt of whitish color at their base, caused by the wicking of silica-rich hot water up from the soil. The geyser basins are like a patchwork quilt of hotter and cooler soil regions, which change over time.

All around us were forests slowly recovering from past wildfires. In the forest fires of 1988, thirty-six percent of Yellowstone's forests were burned. Hillsides of slender, dead trunks stand amid a dense understory of pine saplings, so dense that you wonder how trees can grow so close together. Many will die as the forest grows taller and smaller saplings are outcompeted by larger ones. These forests are often comprised of only one tree species: Lodgepole Pine, *Pinus contorta*, whose cones are uniquely adapted to open and disperse their seeds after a fire.

Gases such as carbon dioxide and hydrogen sulfide are emitted along with steam in the thermal areas, and they are sometimes dangerous. Hydrogen sulfide smells like rotten eggs, but carbon dioxide is odorless. Both gases are heavier than air, and on a calm, early morning with no wind, they can form a layer near the ground and kill an unwary animal, even one as large as a bison. They may also fill small depressions in the soil, excluding air and suffocating small or large animals that venture into the depression. Hydrogen sulfide is so toxic that it quickly deadens the sense of smell, leaving animals unaware of their peril.

Yellowstone's thermal waters are the home of a stunning diversity of thermophilic (heat-loving) microorganisms. The extreme conditions of the first two-thirds of our planet's history are re-created in Yellowstone's superheated acidic and alkaline springs, which have been studied by NASA because of their possible relevance to early life on other worlds. Thermophilic microorganisms include representatives from all three kingdoms of life (Bacteria, Archaea, and Eucaryota) and from viruses as well. All four categories thrive in enormous variety and abundance in these thermal waters, as well as in microbial mats surrounding the thermal ponds and cascading down terraces with the flowing water. The mats come in multiple colors of green, red, rust, and black. They form enormous *biofilms*, aggregations of microorganisms, which secrete chemicals that hold them together. Beautiful yellow sulfur deposits brighten the openings of fumaroles and the basins of thermal springs. The thermophilic bacterium *Thermus aquaticus* was the first heat-loving microbe found in Yellowstone's waters; it became the source of the heat-stable enzyme *Taq* polymerase, which revolutionized laboratory replication of minute samples of DNA. The polymerase chain reaction, which this process is called, has made possible the identification of minute traces of DNA in biological samples from fossils to forensics.

We have visited Yellowstone in two seasons, winter and fall, and have hardly begun to do justice to the wonders it holds.

Powder Keg on the Mid-Atlantic Ridge: Iceland

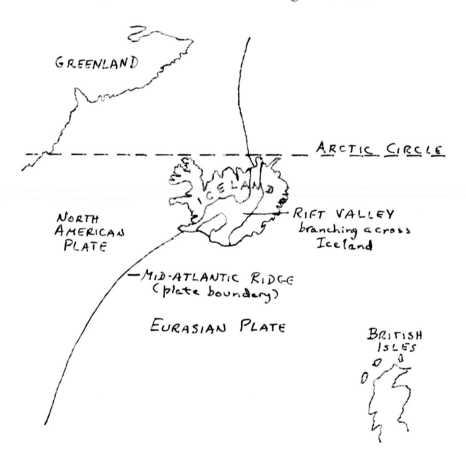

I couldn't see Mary Beth through the dense, deafening torrent of steam. An enormous vent on the warm ground was blasting a wall of steam sideways at high speed, and it sounded like a locomotive going by. Mary Beth was on the other side, and I was filming a movie, hoping she could walk through the steam unharmed. My camera's monitor

showed a whiteout. Abruptly a hazy form appeared, like a magical elf in an Icelandic saga, emerging into view with the wall of steam behind. She had held her breath because of the strong smell of hydrogen sulfide and had taken off her misted sunglasses. We were having fun exploring a geothermal area of the Mývatn Valley of Iceland, ground zero of the separation zone above the Mid-Atlantic Ridge, along which Iceland is spreading apart.

In an active geothermal area of the Mývatn Valley, Mary Beth appears as a ghost as she walks through the steam cloud emitted by a roaring vent (at left). The Mid-Atlantic Ridge is directly beneath Iceland at this location.

Mudpots and geysers appeared all around us, with brightly colored deposits of yellow sulfur on the rocks. Just as in Hawaii and Yellowstone, we had to be careful where we walked because the crust is thin and we knew we could fall through and be cooked. We could walk almost to the edge of one large geyser, named Geysir, which gave us an amazing show; every five to ten minutes, it produced a dome of hot water thirty feet wide, which would rapidly rise and explode into a great burst of spray overhead. We were awed by the power of the Earth to raise several Olympic swimming pools of water a hundred feet into the air. Yet this was trivial compared to the great volumes of lava erupted periodically by dozens of active volcanoes on the island.

A superheated bubble of water, thirty feet wide, rises above the opening of an underground cauldron as we watch it explode into a towering geyser of water. The geyser, named Geysir, was the first geyser to be described, and hurls boiling water over 200 feet into the air.

We had come to Iceland to compare the geology of this subarctic island to that of Hawaii and Yellowstone. All three rest atop some of the hottest spots on the planet. Iceland is unique in straddling the Mid-Atlantic Ridge, a zone of plate separation that extends along the floor of the Atlantic Ocean from the Arctic to the Antarctic. A deep rift valley runs along the axis of the ridge for almost its entire length, and the sides of the ridge are moving apart east and west along the active zone of separation. The ridge emerges at the surface of the ocean to form several islands, the largest one being Iceland. The island exactly straddles the ridge and is slowly growing larger at a rate of an inch or two a year as the two plates, the North American plate on the west and the Eurasian plate on the east, move apart.

This means that volcanism is winning over erosion: more land is being created above sea level than is being eroded down into the sea. Icelanders brag that their country is getting bigger all the time, expanding in two directions, toward North America and Eurasia.

Unlike Hawaii and Yellowstone, Iceland has two sources of volcanic rock that thrust upward, causing it to grow in size: one is the spreading oceanic rift, the other a deep, hot plume of magma rising from the Earth's mantle. These two sources have created hundreds of volcanoes in the spectacular rift valley that branches through the island. Some thirty or forty of these volcanoes have been active over the past century. Icelanders truly live in a land of fire and ice. Some volcanoes are located underneath enormous glaciers, and when they erupt, they melt huge volumes of glacial ice, which form roaring torrents carrying fragments of ice the size of city blocks down into the lowlands and out to sea, wiping out everything in their path. The 1783 eruption of the Laki fissure, which includes over one hundred volcanic vents aligned in a row, killed ten thousand Icelanders and caused extreme weather changes and widespread illness in the British Isles and on the European continent. The fissure eruption released an estimated one million tons of hydrofluoric acid that contaminated Iceland's land, water, and food, causing the disease fluorosis in people and livestock.

Few will forget the recent eruption beneath Iceland's Eyjafjallajökull Glacier in April 2010, which sent clouds of fine ash high into the atmosphere, grounding aircraft over Europe for days. How do you pronounce the name of that glacier? It's so hard that a dozen YouTube sites tried to pronounce it during the year after the eruption. The roughly correct pronunciation is (starting with the letter A, pronounced as in English): *A*-ya-*fya*-thla-*yeu*-kudt (the "eu" in "yeu" pronounced as in the French word *peur*). What a tongue stretcher!

As we drove across the wide Thingvellir Valley in southwestern Iceland, we crossed from the North American plate to the Eurasian one, and someone joked that we didn't even need a passport.

At one point, we fell victim to a hoax played on tourists: that you can stand across a crack in the ground, with one foot on one tectonic plate and the other foot on the other. It finally dawned on me that such a crack is only a fissure in the ground, not an exact transition point between plates. As molten lava from both the mantle plume and the spreading rift valley mix to push the land up and apart, it would be exceedingly difficult to say where one plate begins and the other ends. On a much larger scale, however, the widening Thingvellir Valley is a valid division between the spreading landmasses on either side of the plate boundary.

We enjoyed snowmobiling on the surface of Vatnajökull [*Vaht-na-yeu*-kudt] Glacier, the largest glacier in Iceland and the third largest in the world. The other two are the ice caps of Antarctica and Greenland. Vatnajökull is 3,000 feet thick in some places and extends over an area of about 3,000 square miles. It covers three large volcanoes that periodically erupt and melt large portions of the ice; one of these volcanoes, Grímsvötn, erupted in 2011. Vatnajökull Glacier is a shrinking remnant of the ice cap that covered the entire island during the last Ice Age.

We found that Icelanders are friendly and likeable people who are very proud of their country and language. Most speak English well and were delighted to help us try to pronounce place names in Icelandic. Their language is complicated, with many subtleties of expression, and today's Icelanders can read the Old Icelandic of the medieval sagas. How many of us can read Chaucer's poetry from the 1400s?

Icelanders believe in superstitions of all kinds. There are sorcerers, trolls, elves, ghosts, and "hidden people." There are incantations, spells,

and rune sticks. One guide joked that the U-shaped glacier-carved valley we hiked in may have been created when a huge troll sat down in the mountains. Icelanders explain that they live in a highly unpredictable land and need to believe in magical people whose behavior they can anticipate.

Iceland's rugged coastline protects millions of seabirds, including the Atlantic Puffin, a species which we had never seen before. We couldn't help comparing puffins to Antarctic penguins. Both are "cute" birds that make wonderful photographs. Puffins live only in high northern latitudes and penguins only in the southern hemisphere, except for the Galápagos Penguin, which lives in the Galápagos Islands on both sides of the equator. Puffins "fly" in both air and water, penguins only in water. Puffins have evolved short, stubby wings, which allow them to swim underwater and fly back and forth from the ocean to their cliff-side nests. They cannot maneuver in air as well as birds with longer wings; when you see them flying past, their wings are beating at breakneck speed, like a little engine running fast in low gear. The short wings give them limited maneuverability in air; sometimes they land a short distance away from the nest, where landing is easier, and

In a sweeping panorama, the heart of Iceland, Thingvellir (Þingvellir) Valley, stretches across the divide created by the Mid-Atlantic Ridge. On the left are giant blocks of rock sloping downward toward the center, and in the very middle is a river marking the division of Iceland into North Atlantic and European sides, which are drifting apart at a rate of inches per year. The buildings mark the site of Iceland's first parliament, the center of early Icelandic culture, established in 930 CE.

Atlantic Puffins rest on a cliff edge on Grimsey Island, Iceland. Unlike penguins (which live almost exclusively in the Southern Hemisphere), their short wings allow them to fly, although their flight skills are limited. They often have to land on a cliff surface near their nest and walk the rest of the distance.

walk the rest of the way. They carry small fish crosswise in their bills, sometimes over a dozen, which they feed to their young directly instead of swallowing and regurgitating them. We found that photographing a puffin flying by with fish in its bill was a maddening challenge, and we succeeded only once.

Beautiful flowers adorned the seaside slopes in July and August, making the best of the short summer season near the Arctic Circle. Daylight in July and August lasted twenty-two hours out of twenty-four, and the other two hours were like dusk or dawn in lower latitudes. Icelanders stay up late at night to celebrate the long days and prepare psychologically for the long winter nights to come, when only four hours of sunlight occur in every twenty-four hours. Grimsey, the northernmost island of Iceland, lies astride the Arctic Circle.

In Adalvík Bay in far northwestern Iceland, Mary Beth and I were invited into the summer home of Icelanders on a remote tundra slope. When we hiked past their little house on a small trail, a friendly young woman walked outside to greet us. She had never seen tourists walking on trails in her remote area. She spoke perfect English, and we were told that the sturdy two-story house had been built in the 1920s and is used every summer by the entire family. She showed us around in the cramped quarters, where several children were eating in the kitchen and one adult was still in bed at noon. The long hours of sunlight were enjoyed by all, and many stayed up half the night. Every summer the family came to the bay by boat and stayed for a few weeks before traveling back by sea to their home in the capital city, Reykjavík.

The residents of the small island of Heimaey, just off the south coast of Iceland, were awakened by the fury of volcanic fire during the early morning hours of January 23, 1973, and the event became world news. A new volcano, Eldfell, had arisen from the Mid-Atlantic Ridge right in the middle of the bustling town of Vestmannaeyjar and was sending fire bombs and ash high into the air. Everyone awoke and ran into the streets in their nightclothes, and by the end of the day, all of Heimaey's five thousand inhabitants had been evacuated to the mainland. The volcano continued to erupt and grow, covering half of the town. Five hundred people fought the flow of lava by pumping seawater onto the advancing front. Fire bombs fell around the intrepid workers, who gave each other the advice to look up just after an explosive eruption and "step aside" from the falling rocks. Dark-gray volcanic ash covered most of the town; places where houses had

As the wind dies down, a mirror calm graces the water of a placid fjord in Iceland's remote north country.

The town of Vestmannaeyjar on the island of Heimaey, just south of mainland Iceland, was almost buried by a volcanic eruption in 1973. The slope of the now-quiet volcano is seen in the foreground, looming over the half of the town that was spared.

stood looked like dunes in black snow. Some houses, wrote author John McPhee in *The Control of Nature*, "filled with steam and were cooked until their frames came loose like the bones of stewing chickens." Rivers of carbon dioxide poured down the slopes of the rising mountain, endangering anyone who took refuge in the remaining buildings. After a few months, the eruption ceased, and within a year, 2,600 people had returned and reclaimed the land. A new 700-foot mountain lay at their doorsteps.

We had an unforgettable day on Heimaey, exploring the rebuilt town and climbing the flanks of Eldfell, which loomed high over the 200 homes it had buried. At the edge of the mountain were the remains of homes that had been only partly covered by lava; we

visited one new home built right in front of the remains of the old home and occupied by the children of the same family. The only visible remains of the old home consisted of the frame of a living room window under a collapsed roof, crushed and almost buried under lava rock; the living room had been on the second floor of the original home.

We left Iceland with a deep respect for Icelanders. They love their unique land, history, culture, and language and bravely accept their life atop the powder keg of the Mid-Atlantic Ridge.

The advancing lava from Eldfell Volcano stopped here, leaving intact the frame of the living room window of a home it had destroyed.

Four

North American Wild Places

From the tallest trees in the world to U-shaped valleys carved by Ice Age glaciers, North America offers some of the best wilderness adventures in the world. Mountains from coast to coast invite hiking and camping, slot canyons allow walks up frigid rivers, and deserts beckon with wide vistas to the horizon. Many of these wild places beg for exploration again and again—in winter, spring, summer, and fall.

Dodging Icebergs

Look behind you, Greg," I heard someone say. A black bear was between me and our fish on the grill in Bartlett Cove, Alaska.

The bear moved toward the fire. Not wanting to lose our meal, I foolishly decided I would confront him and walked slowly toward him. He turned and walked down a narrow trail. I pursued him at his leisurely pace. He turned to look at me frequently. Abruptly he stopped, sat down, and faced me squarely. I too stopped, and both of us froze. I decided I should be the one to back down but didn't want to turn around and flee. Instead I walked sideways into the forest, moving back toward our camp. The bear didn't follow. I was a lucky gambler, and we enjoyed our fish.

Mary Beth and I were camping with Mary Beth's sister, Joan Holt, Joan's husband Scott, and our good friend Wini Kessler, a wildlife ecologist in Alaska. We had traveled to Juneau, Alaska, then to the small town of Gustavus at the mouth of Glacier Bay. A bus had taken us and our camping gear to Bartlett Cove in preparation for a kayak trip in Glacier Bay.

We loaded our rental kayaks onto a small tourist boat, the *Thunder Bay*, the day before departure. The next morning we arose at 5:30 a.m. to the sound of pouring rain. Knowing that we had a deadline, we donned raingear and hastily dismantled camp, packing everything into waterproof bags that would fit in the kayaks. The boat trip up Glacier Bay was in rain and mist, and we were worried. We decided to go anyway, hoping the weather would clear. Everyone on the boat deluged us with questions about our plans; we told them we hoped for a week of camping and kayaking in the remote arms of the bay.

Rangers on the boat advised us about risks. Icebergs are everywhere, they told us, and the larger part of an iceberg is underwater. They sometimes roll over and can overturn a small boat if you are too close. The farther up the bay, the deeper they float because the water becomes fresher and less buoyant. These bergs also carried rocks because they came from glaciers, so they floated especially deep.

We disembarked near Riggs Glacier, far up in the eastern arm of the bay. Riggs was a tidewater glacier, within reach of the twice-daily tides in the bay. It was still raining. We hiked over rocks to a place where we could observe the steep front of the glacier and set up our tents. Before darkness set in, we were awed by several calving episodes in which giant blocks of ice broke away from the face of the glacier and crashed into the bay. For a meal before turning in, we settled for snack food inside our tents, hoping for better luck with the weather the next day.

The thunderous roars of calving events awoke us several times during the night. It started to rain harder, and in the middle of the night, we noticed that our tent walls and floor were wet. At one point during the night, we heard some commotion as Wini and her companion moved their tent to drier ground and Joan and Scott tried to divert a stream of water running straight through their tent. Everyone was mad at me because I had wanted to camp next to the calving glacier.

The next morning we took tents down in the rain and again packed our wet gear into the kayaks. Hungry for a good meal, we started out, wondering if we should abort the trip and hitch a ride on the *Thunder Bay* back to Bartlett Cove.

On a misty day, we kayaked among the calved ice fragments of Riggs Glacier in Glacier Bay, Alaska.

We continued kayaking amid floating icebergs of every conceivable shape in the persistent rain. We made it to Goose Cove, where Wini's ranger friend, Rick, lived in a floating cabin. Fortunately, he was there and offered to help us dry things out and wait out the rain. He loaned us a couple of dry sleeping bags for the next night. We found a campsite nearby and set up our wet tents.

Before turning in, I happened to notice that our kayak was missing. The tide had risen and floated it away. Scott hopped in his kayak and retrieved it a short distance away. We wondered what was next.

We awoke the next morning to a sunny day. We celebrated with a hearty breakfast and a leisurely morning discussing our plans with Rick. He told us that he had recently seen a submarine calving event, which we had only read about. Silently a domed bubble had risen in the bay in front of the glacier. It continued to rise, like a mirage, until a white iceberg appeared in the middle—the biggest berg he had ever seen. It was a calving event occurring mostly underwater. Large waves spread outward and are dangerous to small boats.

With heartfelt thanks, we bade Rick good-bye and set off for Adams Inlet, a sheltered cove with an island in the center. The water was calm and kayaking was fun. We found a perfect bluff for a campsite. Because I had first spotted it, Wini called it "Greg's eyrie," named after the lofty nest of a bird of prey. We pitched our tents right at the edge of the bluff, overlooking the peaceful inlet and mountains.

We camped on a bluff overlooking Glacier Bay, which our friend Wini called "Greg's eyrie."

There were no sounds except those of a distant river, gulls, and terns. During our meal, which was cooked over a portable stove, we were entertained by harbor seals, which popped up in the bay below us and watched us curiously. Several small harbor porpoises appeared for a moment and were gone.

I awoke early the next morning to the bewitching calls of Common Loons echoing across the inlet. They were far away, but their yodeling calls filled the air. I have never felt more immersed in a wild place, with no other sounds and the early sun lighting up the pristine Alaskan landscape. No trails marred the wilderness of Glacier Bay; we were camping on undisturbed terrain.

We had only the morning to explore Adams Inlet. We took down our camp, knowing that we had to load the kayaks and leave with the outgoing tide during the mid-afternoon. Mary Beth and I went off on our own to explore a small bay across the inlet while the others started back. Our excursion was beautiful, the water like a mirror. We met the others at Muir Point for lunch and decided to camp nearby on Garforth Island. The weather continued sunny and calm.

We awoke the last day to sunny skies, packed, and paddled out to meet the *Thunder Bay* at mid-morning. We loaded our kayaks and gear on the boat, which continued back up the bay to Riggs Glacier, where we had been dropped off. We realized how far we had traveled on our own. Again we had a deluge of questions from curious tourists and used every superlative we knew to describe our experience. Back at Bartlett Cove, we unloaded everything and prepared for our flight home.

"Wall Street," Pinnacles, and Hoodoos

Before sunrise, by the light of flashlights, we walked to the edge of the cliffs overlooking Bryce Canyon in southwestern Utah. It was spooky approaching the rim in the dark, where a misstep could send us to our deaths 500 feet below. A near-freezing wind blew at this 8,000-foot elevation, making it hard for us to work with cameras without gloves. As we stood shivering, waiting for first light, a dim, red glow began to color the pinnacles and spires of rock formations in the distance. Soon the expanse of cliffs took on a veritable spectrum of hues: pink, rust-red, tan, red-purple, yellow, gray, and white. An expanding band of sunlight moved down the rock walls and onto the scree slopes and trails below. A spectacle of vastness and beauty opened to our eyes, with a virtual forest of tall, thin spires of rock

Rising high above their slot-canyon prison, 750-year-old Douglas-firs spread their crowns to the sun, having shed their lower branches, unlike the Douglas-fir in a more open area to the right. "Wall Street," as this passage is called in Bryce Canyon National Park, must have reminded early explorers of the towering buildings on Wall Street in New York City.

called "hoodoos," sharp-tipped pinnacles, irregular walls, and rock sculptures of all imaginable shapes.

We were exploring Bryce Canyon National Park in the cool of late October. We followed a steeply descending trail to a remarkable slot canyon named "Wall Street." There, growing in tight spaces between huge rock walls, two stately Douglas-firs rose with soldier-straight trunks high above the shadowed recesses of their rocky confines, spreading their crowns triumphantly in the bright sunlight high above. Unlike most Douglas-firs we had seen, their trunks bore no branches below the high level at which they emerged into sunlight. We wondered how, when they were young trees, they had made their way up to the light from the shadows of their rocky prison.

Bryce Canyon—not really a canyon, but a gigantic amphitheater—is a place of superlatives. A canvas of changing rock sculptures takes on a surreal appearance when you hike down the many trails from the rim. The rocks are constantly eroding from the action of rain, ice, and wind, and each pinnacle and ridge of rock is surrounded by a "waist" of tumbled rock fragments. Some of the fragments have been eroded down to sand, which often veneers the trails. If the sand cover is thick, it is soft to walk on; if it is thin, it may make the trail slippery, each grain acting as a ball bearing under your feet.

We had learned that the definition of "sand" is based only on the *size* of particles that comprise it. An excellent book on the subject is *Sand: the Never-ending Story* by Michael Welland. The size range for a sand grain is 0.06 mm (1/425 inch) to 2 mm (1/12 inch); most sand grains are about 1 mm (1/25 inch) in diameter. Any substance—quartz, limestone, gypsum, and even table salt—can form sand. Quartz is the world's most common sand. Limestone (calcium carbonate) comes mostly from marine organisms and consists of fragments of mollusk shells, coral skeletons, and tests (shells) of foraminifera (single-celled planktonic organisms). We had seen gypsum sand, composed of calcium sulfate dihydrate, in White Sands National Monument. We could now see quartz sand in the making in the rock fragments eroded from the sandstone walls and hoodoos.

The cliffs of Bryce were formed mostly as sedimentary layers under the inland sea called the Cretaceous Seaway, an enormous arm of the ocean that flooded one-third of North America in the Mesozoic Era, or Age of Reptiles, one hundred million years ago. The sediments became compacted into rock, sandstone, and limestone, and were later uplifted, then to be eroded by moving water, rain, and ice, leaving the chaotic remnants that stand today. They made us think of gigantic chessmen frozen in the middle of a game.

Elaborate pinnacles and knife-edge ridges, some with windows, have been eroded by wind, rain, ice, and time in the Navajo Sandstone cliffs of Bryce Canyon National Park.

To our surprise, a careful comparison of photos we had taken in 1999 with those from 2011 showed few large-scale changes in the ridges, spires, and walls of the amphitheater seen from Sunrise Point, where details could be studied closely in the photos. Only one "window" in a fin-like ridge had lost its top member, becoming an open two-pronged fork. Other spires and pinnacles still retained identical forms, with large and small pointed tops. The structural stability over twelve years was a reminder for us of how short our lifetimes are compared to the slow pace of geologic time.

Along the Tower Bridge trail, which descended steeply from the Rim Trail, we could see what we called a "ghost city," a fortified mountain bordered by hoodoos that resembled skyscrapers. Bordering the ghost city was a slope of multiple small hills with white tops, which resembled sand dunes. The colors of the hills merged from gray to yellow to pink, orange, and pink again, creating a color palette that seemed like an oversaturated Photoshop image. Isolated hoodoos stood here and there like lost wanderers.

Growing in this desert landscape were three species of pines: Ponderosa, Limber, and Bristlecone, the last looking like a strange plant-form from Mars with curved branches and an overall bottle-brush appearance. This species of Bristlecone, *Pinus longaeva,* boasts the oldest living trees on the planet, with one tree reaching an age of just under 5,000 years in the White Mountains of eastern California.

Snow fell during our last morning in Bryce, dusting the rock sculptures with white caps. It was time for winter to set in at this high elevation. We knew that ice would form in the rocks and hasten their erosion—*slowly*, over the ponderous pace of geologic time.

Sheer Cliffs, Dizzying Heights

In 2009, a woman fell a thousand feet from Angels Landing to her death. It was one of about a half-dozen fatal falls that have been reported from that high destination on a popular trail in Utah's Zion National Park.

Condolences flowed into the media after her death. Many messages were from park visitors who had hiked the trail, some many times. A few complained that the US National Park Service should make the trail safer. Most, however, argued that although the trail is dangerous, the risks are obvious to hikers, and the trail should be left as it is. One correspondent reminded readers that millions have hiked the trail safely and that we do more dangerous things every day.

The Angels Landing Trail ends with a perilous knife-edge ridge that falls away on both sides, followed by a high mountain platform at 1,488 feet above the Virgin River at its base. It provides a breathtaking view of Zion Canyon. Support chains are anchored in the rock, but some sections of the knife-edge ridge lack them. With my fear of heights, I stopped short of the final challenge, as did Mary Beth, although she dared to go a bit farther than I did.

Walter's Wiggles is an unforgettable feature of the Angels Landing Trail. A marvel of human engineering on the face of a cliff, Walter's Wiggles is a series of twenty-one tight switchbacks built into the near-vertical cliff just before Scout Lookout, the turnaround point for acrophobic hikers like me. Drainage pipes are buried beneath the trail's switchbacks. We were at a loss to explain how mere mortals could have constructed this trail on the side of a mountain.

When we first drove into Zion, we needed only one look at the mountains to know that we had entered a world of deeper canyons and more massive rock formations than we had just marveled at in Bryce. Enormous valleys and mountains surrounded us as we approached the mile-long tunnel blasted through rock. The crust of Earth appeared as if it could sink under the weight of these mighty monoliths.

These majestic mountains are formed of aerially deposited sand. Originally sand dunes, the mountains comprise the largest known dune system in the geologic record of North America. The cliffs are formed of quartz sand grains cemented with calcium carbonate, silica, and hematite. Hematite, or iron oxide, is responsible for their rust-red color, sometimes bordering on brilliant magenta-red when manganese is also present. The Navajo Sandstone erodes into silica sand, like that in Bryce.

A hike in the Virgin River gave us a harrowing experience with a slot canyon. The icy-cold water sometimes came up above our knees, and the cobblestones underfoot were slippery. We wore dry suits and neoprene boots and carried walking poles. The upstream walk led us into the Zion Narrows, a passage between high walls that became narrower as we advanced. With great care, we managed to walk through wondrous canyons with shafts of sunlight breaking through, without slipping or falling in the river. We made detours around gigantic slabs of rock that had fallen from the cliffs. Our voices echoed from the walls. We remembered warnings we had been given of periodic, sudden floods of the river that have drowned hikers surrounded by near-vertical walls. We felt safe because no reports of rainstorms had been made for weeks before our hike. Such storms can produce virtual tsunamis of water flowing into the river from the mountains, and a slot canyon offers little opportunity for escape. During the return trip downstream, we quickly learned new walking skills as the fast-flowing water pushed our feet forward.

The Echo Canyon Trail was the highlight of our trips to Zion. We had remembered it from our first trip to the park in 1999, and, except for one detail, it was exactly the same in 2011: a stunning passage through deep and exotic rock canyons. The one detail was the number of people on the trail, which had multiplied by a factor of at least three. Surprisingly, the constant presence of others was only a small distraction from the awesome experience. The trail is bordered by cliffs on either side and is thus relatively immune to environmental impact by hikers. The cliffs are unbelievable sights: great walls of stone, smoothly polished, with linear and curvilinear fractures all the way up, caused by exfoliation of fragments of Navajo Sandstone breaking off the wall from time to time. The canyon walls are so tall and confined that they are mostly in shadow all day long. Their reddish color glows like an

A massive wall of Navajo Sandstone rises almost vertically above the Echo Canyon Trail in Zion National Park. The wall glows like an ember, lit by sunlight reflected from the opposite wall of the canyon.

ember when the opposing wall is struck by sunlight. Stone arches in the throes of birth are frozen on the walls; as flakes of rock break away, the arches are enlarged. If they are high enough on the wall, they may ultimately enjoy full arch formation as the wall erodes away behind them. In most cases, we saw only the early beginnings of arches called "protoarches," many of which were nested one inside another for as many as nine together.

In October, there were broad brushstrokes of scarlet red from bigtooth maples and yellow from Gambel oaks, high on the fractured cliffs. Some trees grew on narrow ledges etched from the great wall. Life must be short for these plants, sharing a brief window in time before their deceptive terra firma breaks away to join the scree slopes hundreds of feet below.

We were approached at a trailhead parking lot by a young couple with climbing gear. They asked for a ride to the beginning of a trail higher up on the road. We gladly accommodated them and learned that they planned to rappel down the sandstone cliffs into a canyon that provided access to the "Subway," a striking erosional feature of the Virgin River, which has carved most of the Zion landscape. We knew from photographs that the Subway was an open tunnel eroded by running water in a slot canyon, where the lowest sedimentary layer had been eroded back by running water and now had curved sides like a tunnel. Since this layer of rock was softer, it was more easily eroded than the layer above. It is reached by a difficult trail and is visited by intrepid hikers from around the world. The trail does not require rappelling down a cliff, as our friends had set out to do.

After they left us, we hiked along an easy trail, the Northgate Peaks Trail, to an overlook where a checkerboard pattern was etched over an entire mountain face. It was a striking pattern that we have seen only in Zion, and to our knowledge, the geologic explanation remains elusive.

We used lightweight trekking poles in Zion to improve our traction when climbing and descending steep trails. We encountered a veteran hiker in his eighties who was using poles like ours. He beamed and exclaimed, "I've got four-wheel drive!"

While we were in Utah, we wanted to find a special scenic viewpoint called Teardrop Arch in Monument Valley. We hired a local Navajo man, Gary, to ride with us and guide us to this rock window, through which we could see the buttes and mesas that have served as a backdrop for movies and commercials. Gary directed us through sandy back roads to the site, which we would have never found by ourselves. Without four-wheel drive, we could have never made it through the sand. The sun was setting on a perfectly shaped teardrop opening in the rock wall that framed Monument Valley beyond. We drove Gary back to his home, grateful for his familiarity with the back country of Utah.

In late afternoon, the aptly named Teardrop Arch in Monument Valley, Utah, offers a keyhole glimpse of rugged cliffs in the distance.

Trees that Touch the Sky

A coastal fog had moved in and blanketed the forest. Massive redwood trunks bolted into the unseen world above. There was no sound other than our footsteps on the soft trail; we had arrived early in the morning on the Lady Bird Johnson Grove Trail in California's Redwood National Park and had it to ourselves.

The scene became more captivating as we rounded each corner of the trail, penetrating deeper into the forest. The green of understory plants framed the black-and-white world above, and lavender petals of rhododendron blossoms carpeted the trail. The views begged for creative photography in both black-and-white and color.

Our fantasy was that if we could climb up into the treetops, we'd emerge in a new time and place. The canopy of a large Coast Redwood is like a "thermonuclear crown," Richard Preston wrote in *The New Yorker*. This "deep canopy," he elaborated, is "a world between earth and air."

Most of us will never have the privilege of seeing it firsthand. The climb is a specialized one like no other, and few have mastered the skills. Permission to climb has been granted to only a few; the giant trees remaining after the commercial lumbering of the nineteenth and early twentieth centuries are rightly protected in Redwood National

Sounds are muffled when a coastal fog, with its magical beauty, envelops the Coast Redwoods in Lady Bird Johnson Grove of Redwood National Park.

Park and several California state parks. Coast Redwoods are the tallest trees in the world; one has been measured carefully at 379.1 feet. Most of them are in northern California near the coast.

Between massive trunks soaring skyward, little foliage appears for the first hundred feet or so. Then the first large branches appear, and when there is no fog, the dense canopy is vaguely seen still farther up. At ground level, the trees form a standing army of close-spaced sentinels, most of their biomass preserved in ponderously large trunks enshrouded by a thick and sinewy bark. Coast Redwoods have grown so tall and have been around for so long that it is hard to place their extremes in perspective from within our tiny personal spaces. Big ones date back to Columbus, still bigger ones to the Middle Ages.

When the wind blows and their trunks and branches rub against each other, redwoods seem to talk in grunts, groans, and squeaks. We were reminded of the Ents in Tolkien's fantasy world of Middle-earth. We were told that in high winds, branches as heavy as grand pianos crash to the ground. Such branch falls have been called "widowmakers." An entire tree is sometimes toppled, with the shallow root system rotated high in the air.

The so-called "redwood belt" extends to the sea, ending in the sand dunes of the northern California coast. In coastal forests, Sitka Spruce, Douglas-fir, and Western Hemlock compete with Coast Redwoods for space. They too are giant trees, but unlike redwoods, they thrive in salt-laden winds, dominating the forest near the sea. High winds break off branches and trunks in this exposed zone, even far enough inland where Coast Redwoods begin to dominate. When Coast Redwoods lose high branches to wind, they cope with the loss in a remarkable way: they grow new branches where the trunk has been snapped off, and some of these new branches turn upward to become extensions of the damaged trunk, forming a high forest of "reiterated trunks" above the break. It is like a forest inside a forest high in the canopy. A human climber may become disoriented in this canopy forest of a single tree; one Coast Redwood, measured by the biologist Stephen C. Sillett and named Ilúvatar, has over 200 reiterated trunks. Sillett has spent much of his life studying Coast Redwoods and teaching about their unique biology and ecology at Humboldt State University in Arcata, California.

We were puzzled by the shapes of redwood leaves on fallen branches. Some leaves were large, beautiful sprays of foliage, and others were tiny, green scales. This odd variation had not escaped the notice of climbers, who had written that leaves become smaller and smaller

Mary Beth is a tiny figure in a rare view of a Coast Redwood from base to crown. (Opposite)

Closely spaced Coast Redwood giants grow and die together in a lush alluvial-plain habitat, where the river rises periodically and provides life-giving water. Tall Trees Grove is one of the most beautiful forests in Redwood National Park, California.

the higher they grow on the tree. Even stranger, the leaves of redwood saplings growing in canopy soil high on the trees were large, like lower leaves on the host trees.

We weren't surprised that Sillett had studied this anomaly. As a tree grows taller, he concluded, water becomes harder and harder to move from the roots up to the high leaves. Water is pulled up by capillary action, and the long column of water is held together by bonds between water molecules. As the column becomes longer and longer, its own weight slows it down, and the high leaves suffer. A redwood sapling growing in canopy soil, on the other hand, has only a short distance to move water from its roots to its leaves and grows full-sized leaves. We wished that we could climb up and see all of this for ourselves.

There is no end to surprises with Coast Redwoods. Researchers discovered that a redwood tree can have a "stroke." If an air bubble enters the thin column of water being raised to the top of the tree, it can block the flow of water and kill the top of the tree, just as an air bubble, or any other embolus, such as a blood clot, can block the flow of blood to an organ in an animal's body.

Canopy soil accumulates in the crotches of branches and pockets in the bark high in the tree. It forms from windborne dirt particles, fallen leaves, lichens, and other debris and can be several feet deep in a large tree. We have seen canopy soil in branch falls in the tropics. In redwoods, it supports the growth of many different plants that form a miniature forest high up. Together with an army of reiterated trunks, the canopy must indeed be like a forest within a forest.

Lichens of many varieties grow on the bark and branches and have been studied by Sillett's wife, Marie Antoine. The two researchers have formed a team, along with many of their students at Humboldt State University, for studying and conserving the few remaining Coast Redwood habitats.

Downed trunks litter the forest floor. Trying to make your way across the forest floor becomes an exhausting game of judgment. This is especially true on steep slopes, where you literally have to climb over trunks jumbled together like piles of sticks. On the Damnation Trail in Del Norte State Park, so named because of the long, steep trail from beach to high forest, we encountered a lone hiker who abruptly appeared out of the forest and asked us, "Where am I?" She had ventured off-trail in hopes of making a shortcut while hiking up from the beach and had lost her way. She had clambered over fallen logs and high scrub on the steep uphill slope and was frightened and exhausted. We told her where she was, and after a short rest, with great relief, she continued her way back to the trailhead. Her off-trail experience was made all the more difficult by the slow decay of fallen redwood trunks; a trunk may last almost as long as the living tree from which it came. The trunk may also serve as a "nursery log" for other trees to grow on, providing soil and nutrients.

A "fairy ring" of new trees forms around the trunk of some old trees, born from burls at the base. The stump of a felled tree may be encircled by over a hundred sprouts, some of which survive and create a ring of new trees. Many are genetically identical to the parent tree, so a redwood's lifetime may sometimes be several times that of a single tree.

Julia "Butterfly" Hill, a young woman in her twenties, lived in a Coast Redwood tree named Luna for two years, from December 1997 to December 1999. Protesting the clear-cutting of redwood forests in northern California by the Pacific Lumber Company, she lived on platforms 180 feet up in the tree. Friends and supporters provided her with food and water, which she hauled up by rope. She learned to free-climb in the tree crown without rope or harness, "feeling" the tree and learning to negotiate trunks, branches, handholds, and footholds. She climbed in her bare feet, the soles of which she left unwashed so that sap on her skin would help with traction. In her book, *The Legacy of Luna*, published in 2000, she described her hardships, which included rain, cold, wind, lightning, harassment, blockade of her food supply by loggers, felling of nearby trees, and even threats to cut her tree down while she was high on the branches. She became a celebrity, and an agreement was finally arranged with the lumber company to spare the tree.

Mary Beth found the perfect home base from which to visit the redwoods in northern California—a rental home overlooking the bay in the little town of Trinidad. We awoke each morning to the distant ring of a bell coming from the foggy bay, accompanied by the song of a nearby Hermit Thrush. The town is built on the slopes overlooking the bay and offers a path up a promontory that overlooks the ocean. The town is small enough to walk everywhere, with a friendly grocery store from which we stocked our kitchen.

For the last few days of our trip, we rented a cabin built at the edge of the redwood forest. One giant redwood stump, harboring a small forest in its rotting core, dwarfed the cabin. One evening, as we were enjoying the outdoor hot tub, we looked up at a dark night sky with stars that shone like brilliant sword points from the zenith down to the forest horizon on all sides. Here, on the outskirts of Trinidad, light

The massive stump of a Coast Redwood dwarfs our rental cabin on the outskirts of Trinidad, California.

pollution was nonexistent. Not even a weak glow could be seen on the horizon in any direction. Overhead the Big Dipper was perfectly framed by redwood crowns.

Although Coast Redwoods are the world's tallest trees, they are not the most massive ones. That distinction belongs to the Giant

The most massive trees on Earth, Giant Sequoias reach for a snowy sky in Sequoia National Park, viewed from ground level with a fish-eye lens.

The ponderous trunk of a Giant Sequoia looms behind two perfectly shaped Christmas trees as snow falls in Sequoia National Park.

Sequoia, a close relative, found in the Sierra Nevada Mountains of California. These giant trees start out as humble seeds, as small and lightweight as oat flakes. Most groves of Giant Sequoias are on the western slopes of these mountains in Sequoia and Kings Canyon National Parks. The state of California is rightly proud of having the tallest and the largest trees on Earth.

We visited Sequoia National Park the following winter and snowshoed among the titans. Their deep-red trunks added vivid color to the snowy landscape. A deep silence enveloped us in a peaceful world.

Coast Redwoods and Giant Sequoias are commonly called "redwoods" or "sequoias," although they are different species. The Coast Redwood, *Sequoia sempervirens*, holds the record for height, 379.1 feet, but the diameter at breast height (DBH) of the Coast Redwood maxes out at about twenty-eight feet. The largest Giant Sequoia, *Sequoiadendron giganteum,* reaches thirty-five to forty feet DBH but tops out at a height of 311 feet. The largest existing Giant Sequoia, the General Sherman, owes its record mass not only to its base diameter but also to a trunk that tapers only slightly as it rises to about half its full height. It is a star attraction in Sequoia National Park.

Another difference between the two species is their natural habitat. Coast Redwoods grow in mixed-species forests within twenty miles of the northern California and Oregon coasts, whereas Giant Sequoias form groves with very few other tree species in the Sierra Nevada Mountains of California.

Both species of "redwoods" live to ages that we can hardly imagine. Verna R. Johnston in *Giants in the Earth: the California Redwoods* wrote poignantly, "A three-thousand-year-old sequoia, the same solitary individual, lives on and on—through one thousand generations of chipmunks, seven hundred and fifty generations of woodpeckers, six hundred generations of deer, and fifty generations of humans."

The Whitest Sand

"You can't follow your tracks back," we had been told, "if the wind is blowing." We were climbing a sand dune in White Sands National Monument in New Mexico just before sunrise. There was no wind, and we could even follow our footprints from our sunset walk the evening before. At the dune summit, we watched the sun creep above the opposite horizon, casting long shadows across the sand. The sun rose slowly, bringing the dune ripples into sharp focus. We were alone in a vast landscape, a 360-degree canvas of orange sand and blue shadow. For a moment, it seemed as if we were on snow-covered hills and could ski down the nearest slope.

As the sun rose, larger features of the dunes came into focus, including overhanging crests that looked like frozen waves in turbulent surf. As the wind blew gently up the dune slopes, particles of gypsum sand were blown over the crest and down the steep dune face, forming little "avalanches" of sand. Grains move efficiently by a process called saltation, in which one grain lands on another and catapults it into the air.

The sand looked like snow because it is gypsum sand, made of calcium sulfate crystals, which are pure white. Most sands of the world

A whispering quiet envelops pristine sand dunes as seen from the top of a gypsum dune in White Sands National Monument.

are made of quartz (silica); these grains of sand in White Sands were about the same size and felt the same to our bare feet. Gypsum sand dunes occur in only a few parts of the world; White Sands preserves the largest gypsum-dune habitat on Earth. Photos from spacecraft orbiting Mars suggest that gypsum dunes may be more common on that planet than on Earth.

With steady winds, the gypsum dunes actually migrate, covering plants that grow in the sheltered interdune valleys where ground water is close to the surface. Some plants are covered by sand and die, but one plant, the soaptree yucca, has a remarkable adaptation. As it is being slowly smothered by an advancing dune, it starts elongating its stem at a high growth rate, often keeping up with the rising level of sand. When the dune has "gone by" and its level begins to subside, the elongated yucca stem may be surrounded by a tall pedestal of sand. The pedestal may persist for weeks because of the slight cementing of gypsum by rainwater, not possible with quartz sand. As the structure erodes, the yucca's stem, up to thirty feet long, is exposed. We found a partially eroded pedestal still holding up a surviving soaptree yucca

A winner, this soaptree yucca kept pace with the sand dune that has now moved past. A rain-hardened sand pedestal is being slowly eroded away, lit by the soft, warm light of dusk.

with a stem extending fifteen feet down to the dune surface and to an unknown depth to the water table below.

On the dunes, we found many soaptree yuccas that must have grown fast to avoid a sandy burial. Only their long, narrow leaves showed above the sand. At the crest of one dune, we even found the top branches and green leaves of a cottonwood tree, most of which was far below the sand surface.

Out of the corner of her eye, Mary Beth caught a glimpse of a small, ghostly animal scampering away as we walked among tufts of grass in a low interdune area. "It's our white lizard," she whispered. We froze to get a better look at it: indeed it was the blanched form of the lesser earless lizard that we had been looking for. It was almost perfectly white, about four inches long, and well camouflaged on the white sand. Its closest relatives, we had read, are dark-brown forms of the same species that live a short distance away in the darker sands of the surrounding Chihuahuan Desert. Over the six to ten thousand years that White Sands has existed, the lizards living in the dunes had changed their color and body shape. These changes were found to be associated with actual genetic mutations, as researcher Erica B. Rosenblum of the University of California at Berkeley told me. The genetic changes include mutation of a gene with a key role in producing melanin, a dark pigment. Dr. Rosenblum found that the lizards show a sexual preference for light-colored mates, suggesting that sexual selection has joined natural selection in adapting them to their new environment.

I recalled that Darwin's finches, like these lizards, have made rapid, real-time adaptive changes in response to variations in rainfall and availability of different foods in the Galápagos Islands. I started to mention this to a member of the White Sands staff until my gaze happened to fall on the cover of their latest newsletter. The headline read: "The Galápagos Islands of North America." The comparison was apt.

Exploding above the sand, the topmost leaves of soaptree yuccas grow fast toward the light as a moving sand dune buries the plants.

Camouflaged to match the white sands of its home, the bleached earless lizard has evolved from a dark-brown ancestor in the few thousand years since its new home was created.

Animal tracks cover the dunes and challenge one's skills at identification. The Visitors' Center has a sand table for kids and adults, with handheld stamps of animal footprints that can be pressed into the sand. We made kit-fox footprints in the sandbox that looked identical to ones we had photographed crossing the crest of a large dune. Kit foxes are among the charismatic animals at White Sands, but they are wary and seldom seen.

At sundown, the white dunes became painted again with an orange glow, and the surface ripples were sharply outlined in their chaotic pattern. The ripple lines reminded me of a maze, with lines joining, separating, changing to a different track, and coming to a blind end in some places. I was mesmerized by them and wondered if the pattern is random and how we might find out. Could one reproduce them with a computer algorithm? I had little time to ponder such questions because the sun was going down fast. I could only try to capture the ripples in photographs.

After the sun went below the mountains, a cool wind began to blow. It was time to walk through the soft, darkening sand back to the road.

One month later, in December, we heard that it had snowed in White Sands. We spoke with excited naturalists at the Visitors' Center, who told us that the snow appeared even whiter than the sand and had transformed the dunes into a different world.

A Desert with Views to Forever

High on the Emory Peak trail of Big Bend National Park in southwestern Texas, we heard the distinct chirp of a mountain lion and froze in our tracks. Nothing moved. We proceeded along the trail with caution, looking at every bush, but never caught a glimpse of our predator. The next day we learned from rangers that a mountain lion had indeed been spotted in that exact part of the trail the day before. We had probably been watched.

What should we have done had there been a confrontation? Stand our ground, open our jackets, and raise our arms, trying to look as large as possible, just as with an African lion. Remain facing the animal. Never run away. Move and stay close together, especially with children, and pick up a small child, bending at the knees. Avoid *bending over* to pick up anything. Then move slowly away, facing the animal. Be ready with a can of pepper spray. If attacked, we should use anything as a shield, such as a backpack. Strike back with tripod or trekking poles and aim for the head, especially the eyes. Fortunately, attacks on humans are rare.

Big Bend National Park, with its "sky island" of the Chisos Mountains in the Chihuahuan Desert of North America, was filled with the colors of wildflowers when we first visited after spring rains. In stark contrast, it was extremely dry when we visited in April 2011. There had been little rain for several years, and the desert was unusually quiet, with few insects buzzing, no caterpillars on the plants, and few birds to be seen. Prickly pear cacti sported thin, dry pads not bloated with water as during a normal spring. The hot midday sun brought temperatures in the high nineties, even in the highlands of the Chisos Basin. Few flowers were in bloom, even though it was the time of year for floral displays all over the desert.

Brightly colored Mexican Jays were common and were uncharacteristically "friendly," coming right up to us on a trail when we crackled plastic-food wrappings between our fingers. They had learned to associate the sound with handouts from hikers. They perched for photos only a few feet away.

At night by our cabin in the Chisos Basin, a striped skunk and a gray fox came almost up to our door looking for handouts. The skunk drank from a small pool of water on the walkway, raising his enormous, fluffy tail high in the air. He was startlingly beautiful with his all black-and-white pelage. A male black widow spider dangled by a thread near the cabin door. Our good friend and co-traveler David T. Roberts, a keen naturalist, teacher, and director of Graphics and Special Exhibits at the Dallas Zoo, captured it and moved it carefully to the ground a distance from the cabin.

Tall, spindly ocotillo plants defied the drought. They were in full flower, their crooked stems with menacing spines reaching over our heads like a profusion of spindly arms with hand-held scarlet flowers at their tips. There were no leaves on the stems—just thorns. Ocotillo leaves flush out at any time of year when there is rainfall, but flowers bloom in the spring, come rain or drought. They offered splashes of bright-red color to a parched landscape. High winds lifted fine dust and created a haze in the air that obscured the distant Chisos Mountains, at other times so clearly seen that you feel you can reach out and touch them. On a clear day, the impression of closeness is an illusion, fostered by the openness of a desert. With dust in the air, the mountains seemed as distant as they really were.

One especially beautiful haunt was Tuff Canyon, a rugged mix of hills composed mostly of tuff, a whitish volcanic ash offering little foothold to people or plants. Dark basaltic rocks were strewn over the

A blooming ocotillo greets the sun rising behind the Chisos Mountains in Big Bend National Park.

white tuff. A lone, spindly ocotillo, sporting a few flowers, grew on the dry slopes, immersed in the heat that radiated off the ground.

Even during the drought, Big Bend offered a ground-hugging forest of desert plants of amazing variety, with good trails through the open-desert wilderness. We learned to be careful, however, if we walked even a short distance off-trail. Cacti were everywhere, some low to the ground, and others several feet tall. The low ones caught us by surprise as our ankles brushed lightly against them. Thin, almost invisible spines could break off in our skin. The spines were painful and hard to extract, sometimes requiring a sharp needle to pry them out. Some cacti seem almost to jump at your ankles and feet. All you have to do is gently touch the spines, and if they are barbed, they become embedded in skin and relentlessly move deeper. Don't make the worst kind of mistake, which I did—stooping to photograph a cactus and paying no attention to a small forest of spines beneath your butt.

Like the ocotillo, cacti offer the best of both worlds. The claret cup cactus painted the parched desert with local splashes of color. One branched stem of a cholla cactus cradled the abandoned nest of a cactus wren. Threads of nest material were sturdily interwoven with the spines; these spines must have provided protection from some predators, but we suspected that snakes could easily maneuver around them.

John Alcock wrote in his popular book, *Sonoran Desert Spring,* of his fear of stepping on rattlesnakes while exploring the high Sonoran Desert of Arizona. "There is always the suspicion," he wrote, "that the next step will be not on terra firma but on reptilia infirma. . . ." Alcock also advised giving wide berth to the teddy bear cholla, a cactus whose limbs tend to break off when you contact the barbed spines; the separated fragments are like "spiny grenades," he wrote.

Even more dangerous than cacti and snakes is the dry heat of summer. As the sun climbs in the sky, dehydration is a serious threat to desert hikers. Water is lost from the body, not only in sweat but also in air exhaled from the lungs. It is easy to forget how large a surface area the adult human lung has—roughly 750 to 1,000 square feet, just under half the area of a singles tennis court. The lung depletes body water with every breath. A quart or two of water is not too much to carry on a desert hike. As the body loses water, blood volume decreases, interfering with the transport of internal body heat to the body surface. The most vulnerable organ is the brain. As it overheats, the brain may fail to control body temperature and blood pressure, and heat stroke may occur, starting with confusion and escalating to loss of consciousness and death.

A vast expanse of the Chihuahuan Desert spreads out like a canvas in Big Bend National Park, with the rugged Chisos Mountains beyond.

Some plants store water in their tissues, such as cacti, which become "bloated" with water, and some animals have efficient kidneys that conserve water and excrete concentrated urine. Other animals burrow underground, still others enter dormancy, and others migrate. Humans don't have these inborn defenses against dehydration.

The Chihuahuan and the Sonoran are two of the four deserts in North America; the other two are the Mojave and the Great Basin. Around the world, two of the largest deserts are the Sahara and the

continent of Antarctica, one a hot desert and the other a frigid one. What, then, is the definition of desert? Although a bit arbitrary, a generally accepted definition is a habitat where annual rainfall is so low, fifteen inches or less, that liquid water is the predominant controlling factor for the growth and reproduction of organisms that live there. For most hot deserts, adding a little water—for example, around homes and settlements—proves the point. Water enables lush vegetation to grow. An oasis develops like a forested island in the desert.

Painted in early morning light, the slopes of Casa Grande Mountain display two habitat regimes, divided by a sharp ridge: one of a well-watered forest on the north-facing side (at right), the other of a hot, dry south-facing side (at left). More direct sunlight heats and dries the south-facing slope.

We learned some other things about deserts. Some desert plants have deep roots that reach the water table; a mesquite tree can have a taproot extending over one hundred feet below ground. Water storage with a relatively impermeable cuticle, or skin, is typical of many succulents, including cacti and agaves. Giant cacti such as the saguaro have shallow root systems but can expand their stems with water after a rain. Green stems, pads, and barrels do the photosynthetic work of leaves in cacti. The scant shade provided by cactus spines actually cools the plant; the tissues shaded by spines may be cooler by twenty degrees Fahrenheit than tissues in direct sun. Plant seeds, like time capsules, may remain dormant for years until conditions are favorable for germination.

Deserts are special places that will forever capture our imagination and inspire us with vistas that extend to the horizon. With its trails in the open desert and its dramatic, high mountains, Big Bend is just such a place.

Rocky Mountain High

I looked with disbelief at the small remnant of Grinnell Glacier nestled against the continental divide in Glacier National Park. I had taken hundreds of tourists on walks over the glacier when I had been a ranger-naturalist in the park in the summer of 1957. Now, forty-seven years later in 2004, the glacier was a shadow of its former self. And something strange was carved into the thin snow and ice cover of the glacier: large concentric rings, almost like those of a mysterious "crop circle" on the surface. I would soon find out why.

I wouldn't know until Mary Beth and I had hiked back down to Many Glacier Lodge, where a park employee told me what had happened. "Since you were once a member of our staff, you should know," she said. "A man fell into a crevasse yesterday and died before they could rescue him."

As if it were yesterday, I remembered all the details of how I would caution people not to fall into a crevasse that might be hidden by a snow bridge. I had carried a few coils of rope and a pick axe in case someone did. I would stand with my small tourist group at the brink of a crevasse and hold the children's hands as they looked down.

Now the glacier was all but gone, save for a small ice tongue sequestered in the shadow of the "Garden Wall," the high continental divide that rose above the glacier's bed. The ice remnant was large

Hidden Lake hangs at timberline above a stunning vista in the high mountains of Glacier National Park. The limestone rocks in the foreground owe their red color to iron oxide.

enough to hold a few crevasses, and some were covered with snow bridges. I learned that two young men had walked out on the glacier the day before, and one had fallen through a snow bridge. His friend had called for help, but by the time a helicopter arrived, he was nearly dead from his injuries and the freezing cold of his ice prison. He died on the flight to the hospital. The concentric rings in the snow had been made by the wind from the helicopter blades.

The summer months of 1957, when I was twenty-two years old, were a turning point in my life. I had landed a job as a seasonal "ranger-naturalist" in Glacier National Park for the three months between my first and second years at Weill-Cornell Medical College in New York City. In June I traveled by train from New York to Montana, where I saw the Rocky Mountains for the first time. When I arrived at Many Glacier, where I was stationed, I was astonished at the beauty of the mountains. I had never seen anything like this in the eastern United States.

My "home" was a trailer by Swiftcurrent Lake, just across the lake from Many Glacier Hotel. I was assigned the Grinnell Glacier hike five days a week and the geology talk on Wednesday evenings at the hotel. I knew nothing about geology but decided I would learn quickly. To my delight, I was given a two-week traveling course with a botanist, a

The broad sweep of Swiftcurrent Valley offers views of the rugged Continental Divide, called the "Garden Wall."

zoologist, and a geologist from Montana State University, along with two other ranger-naturalist trainees. I learned about the natural history of Glacier, photographing everything I saw along the way. I would use my slides in the geology talk I was preparing. In those days, slides were mailed off to a Kodak processing plant, and they usually came back in a week to ten days.

I learned to identify nearly a hundred plants during my training period: trees such as Lodgepole Pine, alpine fir, quaking aspen, and Mountain Ash, and flowers such as beargrass with its magnificent head of cream-colored flowers, Indian paintbrush, red monkey-flower, bog orchid, and glacier lily. The valleys were like a botanical garden. Large animals were uncommon but included the nimble mountain goat, which I saw clinging to the highest slopes. Hoary marmots were all over the mountain meadows, and some friendly ones came to the hotel to beg for crackers. So did the friendly Columbian ground squirrels, one of which became so tame that a hotel employee could feed him on the top of his shoe, then perform a slow, swinging kick that catapulted the willing squirrel high into the air. The squirrel always came back for more.

I had the unforgettable privilege of escorting a small group of tourists on the all-day hike to Grinnell Glacier. I taught them about the plants, animals, and geology, and everyone, especially the children, loved to learn. I felt like a prince with the children. When I was out of uniform and encountered them in the hotel, some would say with wide eyes, "Oh! You're the ranger!"

One child asked me if he could call me "Greg" instead of "Gregory." "Of course," I answered. As of that day, I decided I liked being called "Greg," and it is what everyone has called me ever since.

I was an avid photographer in those days, and my addiction has never been cured. My equipment was pretty good for the time. I had a Contaflex camera with fixed lens and leaf shutter, one of the first single-lens reflexes ever made. I had ordered by mail an accessory "telephoto" lens and a wide-angle lens, and tested them by stretching a small piece of waxed paper where the film should be and inspecting the accuracy of focus. It was good, so I used them both, fascinated with the new photo opportunities they provided. My images stacked up as the summer went on, and I eventually had some valuable slides for my geology lecture and an occasional plant lecture.

Two days of every week were mine to hike anywhere I wanted in the park. I went slightly crazy deciding what beautiful trails I'd take.

There were hardly any bears in Glacier Park in those days, so there was no danger in hiking alone.

One hike took me across Siyeh and Piegan Passes. My notes, written after the hike, record my trip:

> Aug. 22: I passed through the most beautiful meadow country today in the valley between Preston Park and Siyeh Pass. It would be wonderful to take a girl with me on that hike. The climbing was easy and flowers were everywhere—blue gentians, wild heliotrope, red monkey-flower, sulfur plant, all in bloom. I climbed Siyeh Pass and a great, open landscape sloped gracefully in all directions—dipping down to a meadow, sheltering a lake in one corner, and dropping giant scree slopes down to the lake. The meadows in the valley between the pass and Preston Park were green grasslands studded with evergreen forests and crossed by beautiful streams. But I had to walk fast because it was late afternoon and the hotel was still nine miles away.

My geology talk must have been pretty good by the end of the summer. I got compliments that embarrassed me. One member of the audience, a professor of geology at Princeton, said, "That was a very good talk, accurate, and clearly presented. I'm a geologist."

After returning to Cornell, I missed the high of giving the geology lecture, so I wrote it all up when I should have been studying. One of my paragraphs reads:

> We've covered the entire history of these mountains except for one last aspect. Since the mountains were formed, water and glacial ice have worked together to erode away the land and shape the mountains as they appear today. Running water first carved out canyons where our valleys now stand; then came the Ice Age glaciers, which worked like giant pieces of sandpaper, abrading the rugged landscape down to its present contours, with its graceful U-shaped valleys.

One family with several children stayed in touch after they had left Glacier and insisted that I visit them in Alabama when I returned to

my home in Birmingham over the Christmas holidays. "In our house," they wrote, "the ranger-naturalist has all but replaced the Lone Ranger." I regret to this day that I never visited them.

My trip back to Glacier with Mary Beth in 2004 was filled with emotional memories for me. We hiked the long trail up to Grinnell Glacier, a bit more challenging for me at age sixty-nine than it had been at twenty-three. I had been too long away. Showing it to Mary Beth was like seeing it all again for the first time.

Ever since my first summer in Glacier, I have longed to explore and photograph other wild places, and my dream has come true beyond my wildest expectations. But no place will hold more poignant memories for me than Glacier. "My" mountains, valleys, and wildlife, which I had interpreted for so many with so much enjoyment, were the same, and they felt like home.

The sun sets behind the Continental Divide, seen across Swiftcurrent Lake from Many Glacier Hotel.

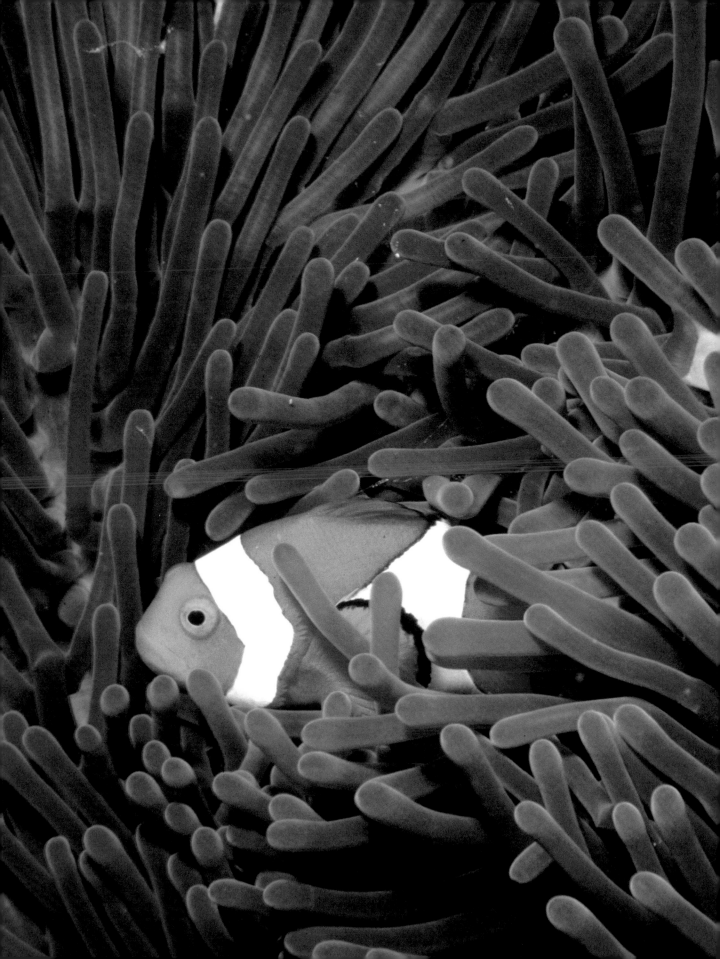

Five

Beneath Tropical Waters

The night was dark, and we could see only where we aimed our dive lights. Mary Beth and I were swimming underwater along the sloping, sandy bottom of the coastal waters off San Salvador Island in the Bahamas, descending carefully as we approached the drop-off. The sea floor was populated with small islands of corals whose polyps had opened wide to feast on the drifting plankton, a surreal sight seen only after the sun goes down. Suddenly I felt a pang of fear as I aimed the light down at nothing but empty water: I had passed over the underwater cliff's edge, and the slope plunged almost straight down into the abyss. I have always been afraid of heights, and this was no exception, even though I knew I wouldn't fall an inch. I marveled at the vast slope beneath me. We checked our depth gauges and started slowly down, recovering our composure and panning our lights across a virtual zoo of marine organisms that lived on the steep wall. We made a safe descent to seventy feet and began a slow return ascent along the wall.

We had become addicted to night diving and were good at it. Our next night dive was on a clear night with a full moon. I could see without a dive light at a depth of twenty feet. The shallow, moonlit reef was an eerie, beautiful sight; I could read my depth gauge by moonlight. Upon surfacing after the dive, I was stunned to see a starry canopy overhead. Beauty and mystery above and below.

Diving on coral reefs is a privilege no one should pass up. There is nothing to compare with this unique planetary experience that might be compared to space travel. You are afloat in a different medium and are exposed to a new world of life. No habitat above water boasts such a diversity of animal phyla in such variety and abundance, from sponges, cnidarians, and ctenophores to molluscs, echinoderms, and chordates. Especially on night dives they are all out on the reef, exposed and easy to see.

We first learned to dive in the daytime. If we were at least thirty feet below the surface, and if there were no strong currents, we found ourselves in a blue world where we could gently direct ourselves up, down, forward, or sideways, as if we were hovering hummingbirds. For new divers, this is an exhilarating surprise; they say things like, "I love it when I get to forty feet because I can go up and down like an elevator," and "I'm free to move in any direction." Drifting over a sandy meadow between coral heads is sublime, with bushy soft corals that look like plants, bending this way and that in gentle currents. Our dive lights, which we carry even in the daytime, light up shadowed overhangs in the reef and may reveal something beautiful, such as a wall of fiery-red encrusting sponges. On the sandy bottom, we might spot a mouth and two eyes belonging to a peacock flounder lying motionless and almost perfectly camouflaged by its ability to match the color of the sand.

On the other hand, shallow dives to fifteen or twenty feet in the surf zone are a different challenge altogether. Divers are shoved around by the back-and-forth movement of the surface waters. Waves crashing above our heads filled the water with tiny bubbles, which made us feel as if we were swimming in champagne. We usually move out to deeper water, where it is calm, as soon as we can.

Once we had made half a dozen open-water dives, we began to feel comfortable with our scuba gear. We discovered that we could outfit our masks with special lenses or learn to dive with contact lenses in place. We learned how much weight to add to our dive belts or our vests, so that we could remain neutrally buoyant, going up or down with ease. We also learned to respect the "tables" or rules of how long to stay at what depth and to use a dive computer. We usually "gave several minutes to the Lord," surfacing early in order not to get the bends, also called "decompression sickness." Nitrogen becomes an enemy underwater because the increased pressure on the body causes more nitrogen to dissolve in the blood that can emerge as tiny bubbles in our joints after we ascend. The nitrogen, not the oxygen, in our air supply is the problem because oxygen is quickly metabolized by the body and does not contribute to the bends.

We learned never to ascend quickly to the surface and never to hold our breath when we are ascending in the water column. Holding one's breath with a closed airway traps air in the lungs, and that air expands as we rise. Trapped air can rupture the alveoli, the tiny air sacs in the lungs, causing an air embolism, the entry of tiny air bubbles into the blood. The bubbles travel to the brain and can leave divers unconscious when they reach the surface. This was nothing to worry about once we learned not to hold our breath; the habit becomes second nature to experienced divers but must be consciously recalled on every dive at first.

We were trained always to dive with a "buddy," remaining close enough together to borrow our buddy's second mouthpiece and air-supply hose or "octopus," if we should need it. I violated this rule several times and am lucky to be here to tell about it.

Because I was a serious underwater photographer, I learned to my dismay that I used up my air supply quickly while taking macro photographs. I would hold my breath while trying to steady and focus the camera, causing me to use more air in the long run. On more than one occasion, I was so determined to get a picture that I pushed my luck and had to borrow Mary Beth's "octopus" to get back to the boat.

We once found a little arrow crab grazing on the surface of a coral head. This beautiful animal has a body that tapers to a point above. I gently picked it up and dropped it in the open water column. It immediately threw its legs up over its head and fell quickly to a ledge below. Fascinated by this "escape" behavior that must help it avoid being eaten by a fish, I asked Mary Beth to repeat the insult to the poor crustacean. I was lucky to get a close photo of it plunging straight down, both eyes looking directly at me. Sorry, little fellow, and thanks. This is my favorite photo from all of our 185 open-water dives in the Caribbean and Indo-West Pacific.

Coral reefs are home to more than four thousand species of fish, many of which display dazzling colors. Why do coral reef fish wear the colors of the rainbow? One reason is that they can afford to be colorful: they have hiding places close by under ledges, if they need to escape a predator. Another reason is that reef waters are crystal clear, allowing vision to be a useful sense for communication. Visual communication

An arrow crab, with its long, pointed body and eyes on short stalks, rests on a coral head next to the feathery arms of a crinoid on a coral reef in the Caribbean.

may serve many purposes, such as a cleaner fish advertising its cleaning services to other fish, a fish seeking a mate, and a fish changing sex. Color may also aid in camouflage on a colorful reef, especially for predatory fish such as a scorpionfish waiting in hiding for prey to swim by. In the open ocean, on the other hand, bright colors could be dangerous because there is no place to hide.

Many reef fish have prominent and wildly ornamented eyes. The pupil, the iris, and the surrounding head may all be differently colored. There are some fish with eyespots on the body, which may cause a predator to confuse the back with the front end; these reminded us of butterflies and moths in the tropical rain forest, which flaunt fake eyespots. Indeed, some of these fish are called "butterflyfish."

Reef fish take on incredible forms. While swimming close to a sandy bottom, we came upon a community of tiny garden eels looking like a forest of long, upright worms protruding from their burrows. They all retreated into the

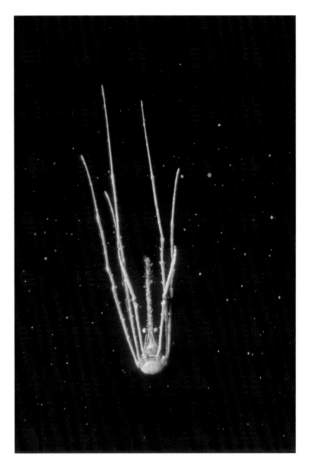

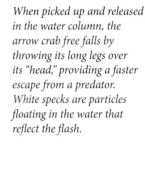

When picked up and released in the water column, the arrow crab free falls by throwing its long legs over its "head," providing a faster escape from a predator. White specks are particles floating in the water that reflect the flash.

A juvenile French angelfish sports dazzling colors as it swims close to the hiding places of a coral reef around Grand Cayman Island.

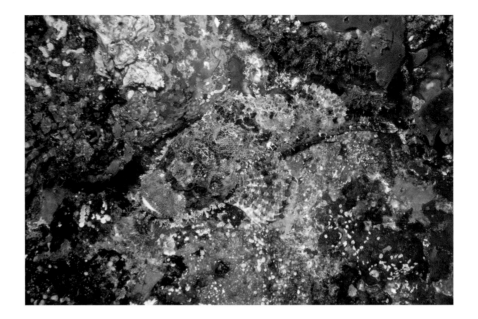

Waiting for a meal to swim by, a scorpionfish lies motionless sixty feet down on Apo Reef in the Philippines, camouflaged with the bright colors of encrusting sponges and marine algae around it.

sand as we approached. Another fish with the most outlandish form of all is the seahorse; aptly named, it looks like a miniature aquatic horse, moving among blades of sea grass just above the sand. Still another is the "pufferfish," a general term for a fish that swells up by inflating itself with water when confronted by an apparent predator such as a diver.

While diving off of Bonaire, an island in the eastern Caribbean, I saw a flounder swimming only a foot or so above a shallow reef. It

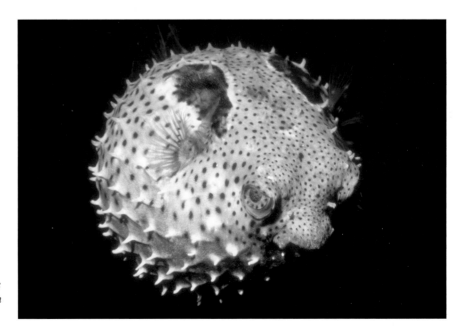

A bridled burrfish abruptly morphs from a little fish to a large bloated ball as we approach it. "Does it blow up with air or seawater?" we were asked. Seawater, of course! We saw this example of an antipredator defense on reefs around Cayman Brac.

displayed a spotted pattern, mimicking the variegated reef substrate. Suddenly it landed on a nearby bed of sand and just seemed to disappear. I stopped. It was right there, partly buried in the sand, with the visible part of its body now whitish all over, without any spots. Its two eyes, both on the same side of its body, and its mouth were barely visible. It had instantly changed color and pattern to match the sandy bottom all around it.

Night dives rival any other wilderness experience we have had. A coral reef at night is like a museum of invertebrate biology, with every kind of animal visible in the beam of our dive light. More phyla of animals are out in plain sight on coral reefs at night than anywhere else on Earth. Corals open their polyps and feed at night; octopuses come out of their hiding places; enormous sea fans or soft corals open their arms, several feet wide, perpendicular to the ocean currents, to catch passing plankton; and invertebrates and fish roam the reef substrate and the sandy bottoms. We couldn't shine our lights in any direction without seeing something remarkable. Night dives are not for the newly initiated but become easy and intoxicating with a little

Bursting with color and helical symmetry, two "Christmas tree" tubeworms remain poised to contract instantly into their tubes on a coral head of a reef bordering the island of Bonaire in the eastern Caribbean. The coral, a "massive" or nonbranching species, is a colony of polyps, all closed in the daytime. They owe their green color to symbiotic single-celled algae that live in their tissues and share the products of photosynthesis with their host coral.

Coral cobbles on the beach of Bonaire are fragments of coral skeletons, broken apart after the death of the coral colony that formed them. The limestone retains the imprints of coral polyps of different sizes. In the brain coral at upper left, so named for its resemblance to the surface of the human brain, polyps formed limestone only on two sides, creating rows and ridges.

experience. After we had introduced some friends to their first night dive, one of them asked us, "Why does anyone ever do a day dive?"

During one night dive off of Grand Cayman Island, we encountered a basket star that had climbed to the top of a sea fan and was holding its long, spindly arms out perpendicular to the gentle current and catching the passing plankton. Basket stars are echinoderms like sea stars or "starfish" but have very long, thin, many-branched arms. The arms spanned five feet, like a giant net. As we approached, even from twenty feet away, it began slowly to fold its spindly arms and crawl down the sea fan. It finally bunched itself up into a tight little ball only eight or nine inches across, near the bottom of the sea fan.

Sharks may be circling close by, out of range of our dive lights. In Caribbean waters, there is little chance of an encounter with a shark, even though they are there. We were lucky to see a harmless nurse shark skulking under a coral head over the sandy bottom.

At night, each of us carried two dive lights in case one should fail. The diver is utterly dependent upon a light at night. In addition, night photography underwater calls for either an assistant with a light or a second light attached to the strobe to light up the subject.

The most frightening moment for me during a night dive occurred after I had made a solitary beach entry off Bonaire, from the dock near my hotel. I was looking for squid and stayed at a safe twenty-foot depth because I was diving alone. At one point, I decided to surface and make sure I was still close to shore; I panicked when I saw the lights of a distant shoreline far, far away, at least a mile. To make matters worse, I turned ninety degrees to the right and saw only dark, open ocean. With my heart racing, I turned fully around and saw the hotel dock a short distance away. How could I be so dumb as to look in the wrong direction?

Another surprise, much less startling, awaited me on a day dive. As I descended from forty to fifty feet, I suddenly entered very cold water. I had passed through a thermocline, an abrupt temperature boundary in the water column, with warmer water "floating" on colder, denser water below. On another dive, this happened when I was swimming horizontally. I entered much colder water, even though I was swimming parallel to the bottom. In the latter instance, I wondered if I had passed through a wave boundary where there are internal waves, which are true waves deep in the water. In any case, it is like walking into a freezer, and I wished I were wearing a warmer wet suit.

Deep cliffs on the seaward slopes off of Grand Cayman dropped down to a sandy bottom at 120 feet, providing spectacular passages between vertical walls that were like slot canyons in the American West. The light was deep blue, the longer wavelengths filtered out by the tall water column above, and a dive light was needed for seeing anything in detail or full color. The dive duration at that depth is short, and we quickly burned the experience into memory. There was little time for taking photos other than scenics, which cried out for a wide-angle lens, especially a fish-eye lens with its domed housing.

We were stunned at the sight of flying fish while riding a boat around San Salvador Island. A large school of fish "flew" on a straight and level course for at least five seconds before dropping back into the water. This represented true flight about one foot above the highest waves. They flew alongside the boat at perhaps twenty miles per hour, slightly faster than we were traveling. The "wings" or expanded fins were a blur. When I saw my first flying fish, I thought it was a low-flying bird. One study has shown that flying fish can stay airborne for distances up to six hundred feet, flying for more than thirty seconds.

A diving medical seminar on Bonaire gave me a deep appreciation of diving hazards. One such hazard is nitrogen narcosis. Called "rapture of the deep," it is the drunken state of having too much dissolved nitrogen in your blood, which bathes the brain. This occurs if a diver goes too deep for too long. During the seminar, we were told of two divemasters who had inadvertently descended to their deaths only weeks before. They had dived to two hundred feet and continued down. They were seen "passing through three hundred feet" by another instructor who survived diving to the same depth and realized the danger barely in time. When the brain is inebriated by too much nitrogen, it is not capable of thinking clearly, and the euphoria only encourages further descent into the breathtaking abyss. One of our instructors confessed

Conforming to the curvature of the drop-off of Apo Reef in the Philippines, fish swim close to coral cover for protection from predators. A fish-eye lens captures the reef's steep vertical drop-off.

that if he ever had a terminal illness, this would be his preferred way to go.

There are some mistakes a diver can't correct after entering the water. One day, after diving down to the reef and finding a beautiful photo op, I couldn't see through the camera viewfinder. I looked at the camera housing to see the lens cap still on the lens. My oversight was so dumb that I didn't want anyone to know. Another mistake turned out to be much more serious.

I almost lost my camera and strobe when I was diving alone on Apo Reef in the Philippines. I was alone because Mary Beth had a mild stomach illness and had stayed behind. My air supply was low, and I needed to surface, but I had let go of my camera and strobe for just a moment to adjust my mask. When I reached for the camera, it had disappeared. I was halfway between the surface and the reef thirty feet below. I searched in every direction, and all I could see was the variegated fabric of the reef. I was close to panic. No other divers were nearby; even if there had been, how could I have asked for help? I had taken some valuable photos on the 36-exposure roll and would lose those and the only equipment I had. *Should I surface and ask for help?* I knew that would be futile. I looked one last time and suddenly spotted it far below, floating motionless against the backdrop of the reef. I bolted down to retrieve it and surfaced as my air ran out, grateful for that one last glance. No longer would I dive without a tethering cord for the camera.

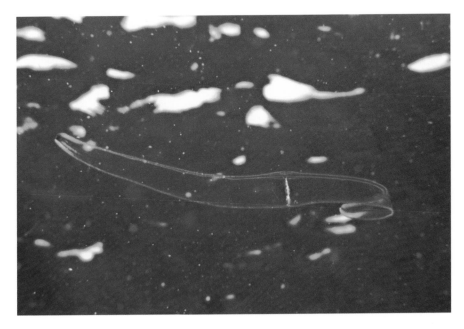

A transparent phantom appears just below the surface—a Venus girdle, a kind of comb jelly (ctenophore) fully three feet long, which undulates as it swims. Sunglints can be seen through its body in the waters of Apo Reef in the Philippines. The animal traps zooplankton in mucus on its body surface and moves it to its mouth in the center (jagged yellow-green line).

The most beautiful marine creature I have ever seen is the Venus girdle, a ctenophore or comb jelly, in surface waters of Apo Reef in the Philippines. These enormous, transparent waifs floated by in the hundreds as I photographed them from only ten feet below the surface. They folded and unfolded with their thin, gossamer bodies spread several feet wide, like undulating sailplanes, then dived to thirty feet and tumbled around before moving back up to the surface. Venus girdles are plankton feeders with "comb rows" of cilia that sparkle in all colors in the sunlight. They are like ghosts that come in battalions and disappear as quickly as they come. There is nothing on land to compare them to; they seem to be made of only water and sunbeams.

Fingers of sand extend seaward off the shores of Grand Cayman Island. From the shallow surf zone at the top of the photo to the reef drop-off at bottom, the light changes from blue-green to deep blue.

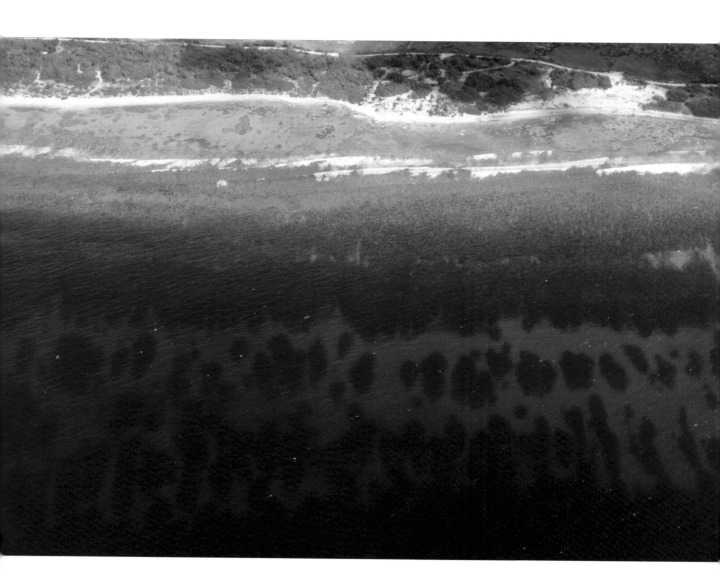

Mary Beth and I rented a light plane and flew above the fringing reefs of Grand Cayman Island. As we flew low over the coastline, we could see the interweaving sand channels between coral ridges that headed out to sea. The color of the sand varied from light cyan to deep blue as the water became deeper. The island was fringed all around with reefs, like a jewel encircled by a sparkling blue necklace.

Some coral reefs cover enormous territory; the Great Barrier Reef of Australia is considered the largest living structure on Earth. All coral reefs are fragile communities, veneered atop a limestone foundation laid down by hard corals, coralline algae, and other organisms. Hard corals are colonial organisms that harbor mutualistic, symbiotic algae in their tissues; the corals provide a home and the algae contribute food by virtue of photosynthesis. The hard coral colony spreads over the limestone substrate with a forest of polyps, whose small tentacles entrap plankton. Most corals open their polyps only at night. It is a new world for those who have never seen it firsthand. The complex fabric of the reef reminded us of the tropical rain forest; in both ecosystems, sunlight is filtered down through a stratified structure, and organisms at different levels have needs matching the prevailing sunlight and shelter.

Coral reefs are in great peril today because of oceanic warming, oceanic acidification, siltation and pollution from land runoff, and human disturbance. In many parts of the Caribbean, up to eighty percent of coral cover has disappeared since 1980. Pollutants from the land have contributed to the growth of harmful algae that compete with corals for space.

For those who have never dived on coral reefs, don't put it off. Learn safe diving; go with a reputable dive company; and wherever you live in the world, consider at least one diving experience on coral reefs in the Indo-West Pacific, where reef biodiversity is the highest in the world. As an added bonus, learn about the biology of coral reefs before you go. You will never forget what you see.

Six

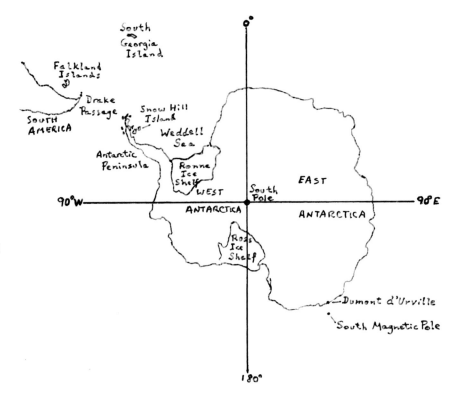

Most of the dramatic wildlife of Antarctica is seen in the oceans and on the shores and islands surrounding the frigid continent. Unlike the North Pole, the South Pole resides atop a thick ice cap, which in turn rests on bedrock. Compass readings are tricky, "ground zero" being the South Magnetic "Dip" Pole, currently just off the coast at bottom right.

Whitecaps and a stiff, freezing wind told us we had entered the Drake Passage, a notoriously rough sea corridor between the southern tip of South America and the Antarctic Peninsula. For two days, our icebreaker, the *Kapitan Khlebnikov*, pitched and rolled. We made frequent trips to the windy deck to forestall seasickness. As we approached the northernmost islands of the Antarctic Peninsula, the wind abated, and we entered the passage that would take us east and then south to Snow Hill Island. There, weather permitting, we would attempt to visit a remote colony of Emperor Penguins just in time to see the chicks still resting on the feet of one of their parents.

On the other side of the Antarctic continent, on another trip, we encountered thick pack ice that surrounded our ship and brought progress to a halt. The captain backed our ship out of its ice prison and headed back to open sea, where the crew chose an alternate destination, the Adélie Coast of Antarctica, south of Australia.

On yet another trip, we had a calm open-ocean crossing to South Georgia Island, a starkly beautiful, mountainous island with penguin colonies spilling from mountains to shore in uncountable numbers. No visitor is ever the same after experiencing this celebration of penguins that covers the land and beaches.

Our love affair with the Southern Ocean, its islands, and the Antarctic Continent was forged indelibly into our memory by these three excursions. The animals we saw live free of fences and remain unmanaged by humans. Their world is still pristine and boundless, as it has been since they first appeared on the planet.

Serengeti Plain of Penguins: South Georgia Island

If I were given ten days to live, I'd spend seven of them on South Georgia. The other three would be getting there," said our friend and guide, Peter Harrison.

There is no other place on Earth like this isolated 104-mile-long island in the South Atlantic. Considered by many the ultimate destination for wildlife viewing, South Georgia is a cold, mountainous strip of land exposed to Antarctic waves and weather and accessible only by ship after a two-day steam eastward from the Falkland Islands. It is all mountains, sea, snow, ice, and carpets of penguins from mountains to shore. A British territory, the island has only one small settlement, Grytviken, and the rest is wilderness. Grytviken guards the grave of Sir Ernest Shackleton, the Antarctic explorer who with his crew made a heroic journey to the island in an open lifeboat from Elephant Island in 1916. Their historic trip was a desperate attempt to reach help after their ship, the *Endurance,* had been crushed by pack ice and had sunk off the coast of Antarctica's Weddell Sea.

South Georgia is part of a mountain range, mostly submerged beneath the Southern Ocean, that unites the southern tip of the Andes with the spine of the Antarctic Peninsula. If you run your finger along the Andes on a map of South America, the mountains go beneath the sea just south of the continent. As they become submerged, they turn eastward and form a broad arc through the South Atlantic, turning back to emerge as the mountains of the Antarctic Peninsula. The entire mountain range, above and below water, is colorfully called the "Antarctandes" by geologists. In its wide path under the ocean, it outlines the

A carpet of King Penguins unfolds from mountain to shore on South Georgia Island. In November the nearly grown "chicks" are losing their brown plumage and are molting to the beautiful black, white, and orange plumage of adults.

Scotia tectonic plate and emerges at the surface to create several open-ocean islands. One of the more remote islands is South Georgia, a small version of Antarctica with mountains over nine thousand feet high.

Unlike most of our trips, this one was with an excellent tour company, Zegrahm/Eco Expeditions, which had organized an unusually long eight-day circumnavigation of South Georgia. Good weather held for the entire trip, and we enjoyed nearly a dozen landings on the island. Two bays in particular were never to be forgotten: Saint Andrews Bay and the Bay of Isles, both with a "Serengeti Plain" of King Penguins reaching from snowline down to the shore. We walked up the slopes above Saint Andrews Bay and had the panorama to ourselves. Some 200,000 "Kings" filled our images from edge to edge, a living tapestry of flightless birds.

We could not have asked for a better guide than Peter, who has written and illustrated several field guides to seabirds. He showed us where many birds nested on the island but pointed out that only two species breed there through the South Georgia winter: the one a flightless bird, the King Penguin, and the other a master of dynamic soaring, the Wandering Albatross. Both birds come to land only to mate and breed. A King Penguin female lays a single egg from November to March (late spring to late summer), and the chick fledges over a year later. A Wandering Albatross female lays a single egg in December or January (early to mid-summer), and the chick fledges eleven or twelve months later. For the rest of the year, these two species make the open ocean their home, but in entirely different ways. The King Penguin lives in the sea itself, swimming from the surface to great depths, whereas the Wandering Albatross lives in the air above the sea, remaining airborne for most of its life and landing on the sea only to feed. I remember how stunned I was to learn that terra firma is not the preferred home of either of these birds. Except for breeding and early development, both birds are almost as estranged from the land as are fish and whales.

The Wandering Albatross is a master of effortless soaring, with the largest wingspan of any bird, up to thirteen feet. The record is thirteen feet three and one-fourth inches, according to Peter. The adult is so large that it looks like a 747 flying over when you are on a boat. On a seaside cliff, Peter led us to a nine-month-old fledgling still on the nest, which showed off for the camera by spreading its enormous wings.

Longline fishing nets are killing the albatrosses. Unlike most animals, Wandering Albatrosses mate for life, if they survive human intervention. Lifelong monogamy is now becoming a luxury for them.

Almost ready to leave its nest for the first time, a Wandering Albatross fledgling has a wingspan of at least ten feet. On the grassy hilltop of its South Georgia home, it tries out the wings it will fly on for the next forty or fifty years.

Imagine, Peter said, that you have not touched land for seven years since you first left. You have flown one to two million miles over the Southern Ocean during those seven years. Now in your eighth year, you are coming once again to land, for the first time since you fledged. How odd land must seem, and yet you are programmed to remember how to get about again on foot. You will court another of your species and form a pair bond that should last for the rest of your life, possibly forty years. Then every two or three years, you will return to land and breed with the same partner for the rest of your life.

Then one year, the male waits in vain for his mate to return; she has died in a longline fishing net. She is more likely than he to meet such a fate because females fly more to the north than males and encounter more fishing boats. The male is now obliged to find a new, less experienced mate if he expects to breed.

The distances over which these albatrosses fly may be the longest of any bird. An Arctic Tern may migrate seventeen thousand miles over the course of a year, but a Wandering Albatross flies almost that far in a few weeks.

A badly wounded King Penguin rests near its colony on a beach of South Georgia Island. The skin of its chest was probably torn open by a predatory leopard seal that barely missed its meal.

For a destination as special as South Georgia, we recommend a circumnavigation of at least five days and preferably eight. Many travel companies shorten the visit to three days. Such a brief window would be a gamble for two reasons: bad weather and fur seals. Bad weather can make zodiac landings unsafe, depriving visitors of disembarking at some of the most spectacular sites. Fur seals come to the island at certain times, and if they are abundant on the beaches, it may be dangerous to land. We walked across several beaches close to fur seals that watched us intently as we passed, but we never had an aggressive encounter. We carried rocks just in case. We were told that on one beach landing, a crew member had been attacked by a fur seal and thrown to one side; he suffered broken ribs and an infected wound. Another guide was knocked down by a fur seal but not bitten; before he could get to his feet, the seal was coming for him again. Another guide hit the seal on the head with a paddle, and both men escaped. On still another occasion, expedition leaders tried unsuccessfully to fight off male seals with paddles and were forced back into the ocean, where they were rescued by zodiac drivers.

Two solutions have been proposed to make landings safe. First, beaches will be monitored carefully for fur seals before landing. Second, if there are male seals on the beach holding territories, a landing will be considered between territories instead of across one of them. The latter tactic has worked on at least one occasion.

The legendary ship *M/S Explorer* had been our home during our first trip to Antarctica. Now, at South Georgia, we enjoyed our second voyage on the "Little Red Ship" painted bright red, which we had come to love. We had brought a copy of our first book, *AnimalWatch: Behavior, Biology, and Beauty*, with us to donate to the ship's library, but our luggage had failed to make the flight with us to South America. We therefore had to buy clothes, coats, and hiking boots in Chile and in the Falklands before disembarking. Many fellow passengers generously gave us their spare clothes. We had traveled with our camera equipment and film in our backpacks, so we had the "essentials" with us.

To our great sadness, we later learned that the Little Red Ship had struck an iceberg off the tip of the Antarctic Peninsula in November 2007. All passengers and crew had escaped by means of a long rope ladder slung over the port side, which was turning upward as the ship made a slow roll before sinking. A legendary home for us away from home was lost, and we shed tears. We wished that a copy of our book had kept her company.

In the Grip of Pack Ice

Long before the Little Red Ship had met her watery fate, she had been our home for our first trip to Antarctica in 1981. We had just reached our destination, the Ross Sea, when we awoke during the night to the sound of bumping and grinding as the ship slowly made its way through broken pack ice. As the day dawned, the pack became thicker, closing over to form a nearly solid cover. Far from land, the ice surrounded us, and we came to a standstill. The captain backed the ship out and tried again and again, with no luck. We received the frightening news that a research vessel about the size of our ship had just been crushed by pack ice not far from us and had sunk. We were reminded of the similar fate of Shackleton's ship, the *Endurance*. With great skill, our captain beat a path back out to the open sea.

Our radar detected some thirty large icebergs within a twelve-mile radius of the ship, none of which was visible because of heavy fog. That was unsettling news. Icebergs are distinct from sea ice; they are fragments of huge Antarctic ice sheets that have broken off and float year-round in the waters bordering the continent. Icebergs can sink ships by slicing them open, as we knew from the fate of the *Titanic*.

We set aside our worries and celebrated Christmas, dancing into the "night." The sun stayed above the horizon all night at this time of year in Antarctica. Under the ship's Christmas tree, someone had placed a life-sized stuffed Adélie Penguin.

Because we continued to encounter heavy pack ice near the coast, the crew changed plans and tried for a landing farther to the west, on the Adélie Coast of East Antarctica. That coast has the highest downslope winds in Antarctica, up to two hundred miles per hour, but it was our only chance for a landfall. Possibly the winds would do us a service, we thought, and disperse the pack ice.

During the next night, the waters again became rough. We awoke at 4:00 a.m. to heavy rolling, which became severe. The whole ship shuddered and oscillated as it smashed down into the troughs of monster waves. I went to the bridge at 7:45 a.m. and spoke to an officer, who said that the battering could damage a ship by buckling the bottom plates. All we could do was slow our speed and keep our heading. As a precaution, we put on long underwear and readied our clothes and cameras in case we had to abandon ship. I put my exposed film in nested plastic bags. We watched and waited.

Another day passed, and we changed course to head for land, hoping that we could find harbor in Commonwealth Bay. The ship was going full speed at 13½ knots. It was snowing outside, and winds were blustery. We were tired of being imprisoned on the ship for eight continuous days.

Again we awoke in the wee hours to severe rolling, thirty degrees to each side, with stomach-sickening descents into seemingly cavernous wave troughs, the result of a force nine or ten storm with wind gusts up to sixty-five knots. At 11:00 a.m., the wind abated and the ocean became calm. We were closer to shore and only seventy-five miles from Commonwealth Bay.

The next morning, the water became even calmer. More and more icebergs appeared as we neared shore; the staff called it "Iceberg City." Finally we could see ice cliffs on the shores of Antarctica.

The weather remained calm and clear. We dropped anchor in Commonwealth Bay, went ashore in zodiacs, and set foot on the continent for the first time. The Adélie Penguins there had probably never seen a human before. No tourist vessel had ever landed there. Almost at the edge of the land was a sturdy wooden cabin half-filled with snow, built in the early 1900s by Sir Douglas Mawson and his men, Australians who were intrepid early explorers of this wild coast. The exterior walls of the cabin were reinforced with at least a hundred small pieces of wood nailed across the cracks between the main boards to keep out snow blown by the fierce katabatic winds.

Mawson and two other men had set out in 1911 from this cabin with dogs, sleds, and supplies to explore the ice shelf far inland. The gripping story of his adventure is told in *Mawson's Will: The Greatest Survival Story Ever Written*, by Lennard Bickel. Only Mawson made it back to the cabin alive. One of his two companions and most of their equipment met their end in the collapse of an ice bridge over a glacial crevasse. During the long, desperate trek back, the sled dogs died one by one from starvation, and the two surviving men resorted to consuming the flesh of the departed dogs, including the dogs' livers, which were rich in vitamin A. Before they could get back, Mawson's remaining companion died, possibly from hypervitaminosis A, a severe illness caused by vitamin A toxicity. Mawson barely made it to the steep slope above the cabin where we now stood, unable to descend the slope for several days because of strong winds. From his

An Adélie Penguin catapults out of the water onto pack ice at France's Dumont d'Urville Station on the Adélie Coast of Antarctica, located due south of Australia. The documentary March of the Penguins *was filmed in the vicinity of this station.*

high vantage point, he saw the last boat of the fall season leave for home, and his stomach sank. The few men who had stayed behind finally spotted him in the distance and were galvanized into action. They climbed the slope and helped him down, and he recovered while overwintering at the station. The story is a legend in the history of Antarctic exploration.

At Commonwealth Bay, we marveled at the enormous floating tongue of Mertz Glacier, an extension of the continental ice cap that flowed out past the land's edge. Huge caves and arches as high as forty feet above the sea had been sculpted by waves in its sides. Zodiac drivers daringly took us a short distance under the arches, where surface waters became calm.

We returned to the ship and traveled slightly farther to the west, stopping a short distance off the coast of France's Dumont d'Urville Station. For a safe passage to the station through the pack ice and icebergs, we followed in the wake of a supply boat. Once on land, we met an enthusiastic band of researchers and enjoyed talking to them in French. They took as many photos of us as we of them because they

Emperor Penguin fledglings, five or six months of age, rest on a fragment of floating pack ice near France's Dumont d'Urville Station. They are now on their own and are hopefully ready to make the sea their home for the next two or three years, before returning to land to breed.

had never seen tourists there before. Years later, this station would serve as the base of operations for the French team which made the unforgettable documentary, *March of the Penguins*. The skies were clear, and we enjoyed twenty-four hours of sunlight on the coast. We took a picture of ourselves at midnight with the bright sun just above the horizon behind us.

We were scheduled to return to our starting point in New Zealand, and the Little Red Ship moved at top speed away from the continent. We were excited to have walked on the ice cap and continental rock of Antarctica. As we left for the open ocean, we passed close to the South Magnetic "Dip" Pole, where a compass needle would wander erratically.

During the second night at sea, we awoke to a familiar, uncomfortable feeling: extreme pitching and rolling. I became aware of a pattern to the ship's movement: there was a deceleration as the bow climbed a wave slope, followed by a sickening plunge into the trough, then a shudder and series of shocks that felt like an undulation traveling along the ship. At the same time, there was a wide rolling motion so severe that I asked the staff what our angle of roll had been: fifty degrees, I was told, the most extreme they had known on this ship. "Everyone get in your bed and put on your security belts," came the announcement. As the rolling continued, we could hear crashing sounds across the ship as dishes and debris flew everywhere. Several passengers suffered serious injuries, and the ship's doctor was busy. I will spare readers the details of our next discovery: our cabin was on a lower level, and the ship's sewage flooded all the bathrooms on that level.

From inside the bridge, I photographed the ship fully tilted, first with the horizon flat across the image, then with the bridge flat across the image. A strange double take.

In the welcome calm seas near New Zealand, the ship's farewell gala dinner was served. It consisted only of dry sandwiches and fruit. We docked and disembarked at the Port of Invercargill of the South Island of New Zealand. The next day a local newspaper (*The Southland Times*, Invercargill, January 6, 1982) published the following headlines:

> **First Tourists at Hut:** Lindblad Explorer passengers have become the first tourists ever to see the hut used by forgotten Antarctic explorer Douglas Mawson—a man whose story ranks higher than Scott's, in the view of the cruise director, Mr. Mike McDowell.

Emperor Chicks "on Feet" in a Frigid Land

The sea was a patchwork quilt of snow-covered pack ice. An icy wind of forty knots was blowing, creating an air-chill factor of minus fifty degrees Fahrenheit. It was uncomfortably cold on the upper deck of the *Kapitan Khlebnikov* even with cold-weather gear. The light was blindingly bright in spite of a sun low in the sky. The ship was frozen in its tracks, unable to penetrate further into the ice. We were still forty miles from our destination, Snow Hill Island, where an Emperor Penguin colony was close to shore.

It was October 2007, and we had hoped to experience the treat of a lifetime—a visit to an Emperor Penguin colony on the coast of the coldest sea in Antarctica, the Weddell Sea. But our powerful icebreaker had been defeated by unseasonably thick pack ice. The captain tried again and again to break through but left only the imprint of the bow in the ice, along with a hint of paint. He admitted defeat, and we stopped where we were.

The crew made a daring decision to mobilize the two small helicopters on the ship and fly passengers to the fringes of the colony. A window of hazy sun and calm wind had opened. In case bad weather closed in, a large tent and provisions adequate for three days were unloaded at the landing site before airlifting passengers. The weather in Antarctica is fickle and can change for the worse in a heartbeat.

A canvas of ice and snow spreads before our ship in the Weddell Sea of Antarctica, with blue icebergs which have calved off the ice mantle of the Antarctic continent.

Leaving its imprint (and a little paint) in the thick pack ice, the icebreaker Kapitan Khlebnikov *backs off to seek an open passage in the Weddell Sea.*

Our ship casts a long shadow over the frigid landscape of the ice-covered Weddell Sea.

Antarctica and the Southern Ocean **151**

The helicopter flight took us over a magical ice-bound seascape of staggering beauty. A vast panorama of sea ice opened up, studded with blue icebergs and covered with a fresh blanket of snow. We landed on a small snow-covered beach about a mile from the colony and hiked up a low hill to an incredible sight. Hundreds of adult Emperors with their chicks stood on the snow in front of the rising hills of the island. Some chicks were still "on feet," others old enough to walk around on their own. They were unafraid of us and often walked over to inspect us. In their genetic code, there was no evolutionary memory of predators resembling us.

Two adults often stood facing each other, with one chick begging for food from one of them. Male and female Emperors look so much

alike that we couldn't tell the sex of the adults. Peter Harrison was our guide, as he had been on South Georgia Island. Sometimes, as Peter explained, an adult without a chick tries to steal a chick from its rightful parent. At other times, the parent of the opposite sex, which had made the long walk back from feeding at sea, was changing places with the hungry parent that had stayed behind. If there are two adults with a begging chick, in most cases both adults are the parents.

Emperors, unlike any other birds, reproduce in the middle of the brutal Antarctic winter. After the female lays her single egg in May or June, she makes the long trek back to the sea. The male incubates the egg until it hatches in August, then feeds the chick on his feet with a secretion from his esophagus, even though he has fasted for three

Reached only by ship and helicopter, an isolated colony of Emperor Penguins survives on the snow and ice of Snow Hill Island in the Weddell Sea. Stormy weather threatens as we photograph the spectacle in a multi-image panorama in October 2007. The chicks had been born in July, in the dead of the Antarctic winter.

months. When the female finally returns, he recognizes her by her vocalizations, and they agree to exchange places. The famished male, who has lost forty percent of his weight, makes his way back to the sea to feed. He returns after three or four weeks and takes over feeding duties again.

This trade-off continues until November or December, when fledging occurs and the chick is on its own. The ocean is closer now because coastal snows have melted and the pack ice is breaking up. Chicks may ride an ice floe out to their new home, the open sea.

We marveled at how natural selection can bring about such adaptations. Emperor fledglings with no open-ocean experience can plunge into the sea; swim with their wings; hunt for fish, squid, and

An Emperor Penguin chick, about 70 days old, is old enough to explore the world off of its parents' feet.

krill; dive to one thousand feet; and come to the surface to breathe, adapting to an entirely new world. When they reach four or five years of age and return to land to breed, Emperors endure temperature extremes that seem to constitute an antipredator advantage, just as Lesser Flamingoes do on the scorching mud flats of Lake Natron, but in the opposite direction on the temperature scale—Emperors at minus 40 degrees Fahrenheit, Lesser Flamingoes at plus 140 degrees.

We spent four hours with the colony, but the visit seemed like only minutes. A harsh wind had begun to blow, and the weather was turning colder. We were told to return to the helicopter and didn't need to be persuaded. The flight back to the ship was again over an enchanted seascape. We had just become the luckiest people we knew.

A Emperor Penguin chick too young to be on its own remains on the feet of one of its parents.

Breeding at opposite, punishing extremes of the temperature scale, Emperor Penguins and Lesser Flamingoes enjoy relative freedom from predators while raising their young.

-40° Fahrenheit

+140° Fahrenheit

For the Love of Wild Places

Nature is defined by deep beauty—beauty in the peacefulness of a dense forest, in the grace of a cheetah running at full speed, in the long winter months endured by a pair of Emperor Penguins raising their single chick. Beauty exists in simple things, such as a flower petal on a path in a Coast Redwood forest, and in complex things, such as the calculus evident in a marine turtle's laying of her eggs at a time when high tides will offer hatchlings a short race to the sea. Beauty is expressed in sounds: the pounding surf on a rocky coast, heavy raindrops hitting large tropical leaves, the song of the Hermit Thrush, and the crescendo roars of two male lions patrolling their territory under a Serengeti moon. Smells can be beautiful, too, from the salt spray of the ocean to the musty aroma of mushrooms, from the fragrance of a wildflower to fresh dirt in a gardener's hands.

Does science deprive us of the beauty of mystery? I find that if I understand something better, awe enhances mystery. A mystery "solved" spawns even more mysteries, and we never cease to wonder and appreciate.

Endless adventure abounds in wild places, which some day will sadly be mere memories from the past. Luckily, they are still here for us to explore. I hope that many will be as fortunate as we to touch the face of nature and light the fuse in others.

Reading about Wild Places

Alcock, John. *Sonoran Desert Spring*. Chicago: University of Chicago Press, 1985.

Bickel, Lennard. *Mawson's Will: The Greatest Survival Story Ever Written*. New York: Stern and Day, 1977.

Brown, Leslie. *The Mystery of the Flamingos*. Nairobi, Kenya: East African Publishing House, 1973.

Carroll, Sean B. *Remarkable Creatures: Epic Adventures in the Search for the Origins of Species*. New York: Mariner Books / Houghton Mifflin Harcourt, 2009.

Dimijian, Gregory G. "Darwinian Natural Selection: Its Enduring Explanatory Power," *Baylor University Medical Center Proceedings* 25, no. 2 (2012): 139–147.

——, and Mary Beth Dimijian. *AnimalWatch: Behavior, Biology, and Beauty*. New York: Harry N. Abrams, 1996.

Dinesen, Isak. *Out of Africa*. New York: Random House, 1938.

Doughty, Andrew. *Hawaii The Big Island Revealed: The Ultimate Guidebook, Sixth Edition*. Lihu'e, Hawaii: Wizard Publications, 2011.

Ehrlich, Paul R., and Anne H. Ehrlich. *The Dominant Animal: Human Evolution and the Environment*. Washington: Island Press, 2008.

Estes, Richard D. *The Behavior Guide to African Mammals*. Berkeley: University of California Press, 1991.

Everts, John, and Marjorie Popper, eds. *Coast Redwood: A Natural and Cultural History*. Los Olivos, California: Cachuma Press, 2001.

Gaston, Kevin J. "Global Patterns in Biodiversity," *Nature* 405, no. 6783 (2000): 220–227.

Goodall, Jane. *Jane Goodall: 50 Years at Gombe: A Tribute to Five Decades of Wildlife Research, Education, and Conservation*. New York: Stewart, Tabori & Chang Publishers, 2010.

Grzimek, Bernhard, and Michael Grzimek. *Serengeti Shall Not Die.* New York: E. P. Dutton & Company, 1959.

Harrison, Peter. *Seabirds of the World: A Photographic Guide.* Princeton, New Jersey: Princeton University Press, 1996.

Hill, Julia B. *The Legacy of Luna: The Story of a Tree, a Woman, and the Struggle to Save the Redwoods.* San Francisco: HarperCollins, 2000.

Janzen, Daniel H., ed. *Costa Rican Natural History.* Chicago: University of Chicago Press, 1983.

Johnston, Verna R. "Sierra Nevada: The Naturalist's Companion," in Peter Johnstone, ed. *Giants of the Earth: The California Redwoods.* Salt Lake City, Utah: Publishers Press, 2001, 10–18.

Knowlton, Nancy. "Coral Reefs," *Current Biology* 18, no. 1 (2008): R18–R21.

Kritcher, John. *A Neotropical Companion: An Introduction to the Animals, Plants, and Ecosystems of the New World Tropics.* Second Edition. Princeton: Princeton University Press, 1997.

McPhee, John. *The Control of Nature.* New York: Farrar, Straus and Giroux, 1989.

Moffett, Mark W. *The High Frontier: Exploring the Tropical Rainforest Canopy.* Cambridge: Harvard University Press, 1993.

Moss, Cynthia. *Elephant Memories: Thirteen Years in the Life of an Elephant Family.* New York: William Morrow and Company, 1988.

——. *Portraits in the Wild: Animal Behavior in East Africa, Second Edition.* Chicago: University of Chicago Press, 1982.

Owens, Mark and Delia. *Cry of the Kalahari: Seven Years in Africa's Last Great Wilderness.* Boston: Houghton Mifflin, 1984.

Padian, Kevin. "Darwin's Enduring Legacy," *Nature* 451, no. 7179 (2008): 632–634.

Preston, Richard. "Climbing the Redwoods: A Scientist Explores a Lost World over Northern California," *The New Yorker* (February 14, 2005): 212–225.

——. "Tall for Its Age: Climbing a Record-Breaking Redwood," *The New Yorker* (October 9, 2006): 32–36.

——. *The Wild Trees*. New York: Random House, 2007.

Scott, Jonathan. *The Great Migration*. New York: Viking Penguin, 1988.

Shackleton, Ernest. *South: The Story of Shackleton's Last Expedition 1914–17*. London: William Heinemann, 1983. Original edition London: William Heinemann, 1919.

Sinclair, Anthony R. E. *Serengeti Story: Life and Science in the World's Greatest Wildlife Region*. Oxford: Oxford University Press, 2012.

Weiner, Jonathan. *The Beak of the Finch*. New York: Vintage Books (Random House), 1994.

Welland, Michael. *Sand: The Never-Ending Story*. Berkeley: University of California Press, 2009.

Wilson, Edward O. *Naturalist*. Washington: Island Press, 2006.

——. *The Diversity of Life*. New York: W.W. Norton & Company, 1992.

Index

Photographs are indicated by page number in *italics*.

Gregory G. Dimijian, MD
Mary Beth Dimijian

Greg Dimijian is Clinical Associate Professor of Psychiatry at the University of Texas Southwestern Medical School in Dallas where he teaches an annual course in behavioral ecology. Mary Beth Dimijian taught elementary school for three decades in Richardson, Texas. They have worked with researchers and field biologists around the world to understand and photograph the Earth's natural heritage and have taught lay and professional audiences about wild places and animal behavior. Their photographs have appeared in *National Geographic* publications, the *New York Times, Time* magazine, *Natural History, Scientific American, International Wildlife, Sky & Telescope, Nature, Science*, and many other publications. *For the Love of Wild Places* is their second book.